コミュニケーションのための やり直し英文法

Fifty Grammar Keys to Communication

Susumu Kusano
Steve Lia

草野 進
スティーブ・リア 共著

中学・高校で習った英文法を完全マスター

IBC パブリッシング

Preface

　この本を手に取ったあなたは英語でのコミュニケーション力の向上への〈Keys〉を手にしようとしています。ここに英語コミュニケーション力を本物にするための50の文法 Key があります。この鍵を手にとって扉を開けてくれることを祈念します。

　グローバル化に伴ってコミュニケーションの道具〈Tool〉としての英語力の重要性が叫ばれています。コミュニケーションと聞いて、思い浮かべることは人さまざまです。従前は大学の授業科目にも「英会話」などがありましたが、現在は姿を消し、「英語コミュニケーション」などと名称・内容を変えています。「英会話」で括られる"挨拶程度"では不十分と考えられるようになりました。

　世間では「文法」しか学んでいないから「コミュニケーション」ができない、と区別し「文法」に責任転嫁をしようとしている傾向が見られます。しかし、正しい文法を知って初めて十分な意思疎通ができるのです。

　Fast-food のお店で、ハンバーガーを注文しようとして、"For here, or to go?"（こちらでお召し上がりですか、お持ち帰りですか？）と聞かれたことに対して、"For here." や "To go." と答えて、無事目的の食料を手に入れるだけでも"コミュニケーション"かも知れませんが、今考えていることが全て英語で表現できて、相手に伝えることができるようになるためには、文法の力が欠かせません。相手が言っていることを間違いなく理解するた

めにも同じことが言えます。中学生や高校生、そして大学生はもちろん、仕事で英語を使う人、あるいは家庭にいる方にも、鍵〈Keys〉を与えるのが本書の大きな Mission〈使命〉です。「今度こそ英語の力をつけたい」と思っている人へのメッセージでもあります。

　中学や高校で学んだ英文法はコミュニケーションを円滑にする上でとても大切な要素です。文章読解や英作文だけに使っていた文法内容を復習することで、無駄なく効果的に英語力をつけることができると信じています。何度トライしてみてもコミュニケーション力が向上しなかった方には、お奨めの内容です。

　本書の執筆にあたり、玉川大学リベラルアーツ学部 准教授 Steve Lia 氏に Listen & Read の会話文と Drills の作成を担当していただきました。お互いに議論をしながら、50の文法項目をまとめ、読みやすく、力を付けやすい内容にできたと思っています。読者各位の実用に委ねたいと思います。IBCパブリッシングの浦晋亮社長にもアイデアの構築からレイアウトなど大変お世話になりました。ここに御礼申し上げます。

玉川大学 リベラルアーツ学部教授
草野　進

How to use this book

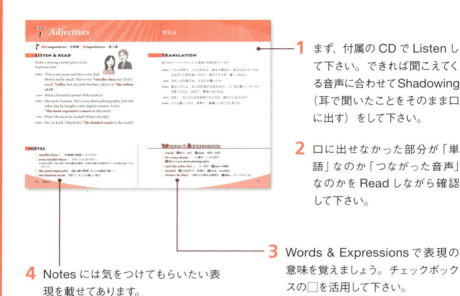

1 まず、付属のCDでListenして下さい。できれば聞こえてくる音声に合わせてShadowing（耳で聞いたことをそのまま口に出す）をして下さい。

2 口に出せなかった部分が「単語」なのか「つながった音声」なのかをReadしながら確認して下さい。

3 Words & Expressionsで表現の意味を覚えましょう。チェックボックスの□を活用して下さい。

4 Notesには気をつけてもらいたい表現を載せてあります。

5 次にExploring Grammarで文法を確認しましょう。Keyの番号とListen & Readの中の番号が呼応しています。「なぜそのように表現するのか？」を常に頭に置いて読んでいただければ、Nuances（微妙な違い）が分かり、実力向上は揺るがないものになります。

本書には30のUnitに50の文法Keysがまとめてあります。英語でのコミュニケーションにおいて必要な項目が網羅されています。これさえ覚えれば大丈夫と考えて取り組んで下さい。

6 実力を Strategies for the TOEIC で試してみましょう。Can you remember? は本文中での確認事項です。Can you guess? は確認事項を理解した上で、考え出すことができるかどうかを試しています。解答はすぐ下にあります。

7 10個のUnitごとに復習問題があります。再確認して実力を定着させましょう。

8 最後にもう一度CDを聞いて、自分の役割を決めて会話に参加しましょう。全部のLine（台詞）が言えるようになれば完璧です。読者諸兄のコミュニケーション力への賛助ができれば幸甚です。

Contents

Preface ·· 2
How to use this book ·· 4
Meet the characters ··· 8

✦ ✦ ✦ ✦

Unit 1	**Adjectives**	形容詞 ················· 10
Unit 2	**Adverbs of frequency & Articles**	頻度を表す副詞と冠詞 ················· 16
Unit 3	**Auxiliary verbs**	助動詞 ················· 24
Unit 4	**Conditionals (1)**	条件文 (1) ················· 32
Unit 5	**Conditionals (2)**	条件文 (2) ················· 38
Unit 6	**Conjunctions**	接続詞 ················· 46
Unit 7	**Future forms**	未来形 ················· 52
Unit 8	**Verbs (1)**	動詞 (1) ················· 58
Unit 9	**Look**	～に見える ················· 66
Unit 10	**Modal verbs (1)**	助動詞 (1) ················· 72

Review 1 ·· 78

Unit 11	Modal verbs (2)	助動詞 (2)	82
Unit 12	Nouns (1)	名詞 (1)	88
Unit 13	Nouns (2)	名詞 (2)	94
Unit 14	Participles	分詞	100
Unit 15	Passive voice	受動態	106
Unit 16	Phrasal verbs	句動詞	114
Unit 17	Prepositions	前置詞	124
Unit 18	Pronouns	代名詞	132
Unit 19	Questions	疑問文	140
Unit 20	Relative pronouns	関係代名詞	148
Review 2			154

Unit 21	Reported speech	間接疑問文	158
Unit 22	Subjunctives	仮定法	164
Unit 23	Tenses (1)	時制 (1)	170
Unit 24	Tenses (2)	時制 (2)	176
Unit 25	Tenses (3)	時制 (3)	184
Unit 26	Tenses (4)	時制 (4)	192
Unit 27	Time expressions (1)	時間表現 (1)	198
Unit 28	Time expressions (2)	時間表現 (2)	204
Unit 29	Verbs (2)	動詞 (2)	210
Unit 30	Verbs (3)	動詞 (3)	218
Review 3			224

Meet the characters

A) Keiko, John, (Makoto)

Keiko and **John** are a young couple. They move to a new apartment in Tokyo. Keiko is from Yokohama and John is from Los Angeles, USA. John works for a trading company in Tokyo. **Makoto** is John's business colleague.

Keiko

John

Makoto

B) Maki, Kate, (Ken, Sally)

Maki

Kate

Maki and **Kate** are university students. Kate is from San Francisco, USA. She is in Japan on a one-year study program. She meets Maki at university and they become best friends. They rent an apartment in Tokyo together. **Ken** is Maki's old high school friend. **Sally** is Kate's friend, visiting from America.

Sally

Ken

C) Trevor, Angela, Emily, Georgie, (Eiji, Tim)

Trevor and **Angela Brown** are Canadian tourists based in the UK. They are on a two-week holiday in Japan with their daughter, **Emily** (16) and their son, **Georgie** (12). Trevor runs a computer company in London, England. **Eiji** is a writer from Kyoto whom Trevor meets on the train. Trevor meets **Tim**, a university lecturer from the United States, in a pub.

Trevor

Emily

Georgie

Angela

Eiji

Tim

▶ Stories in which the characters appear.

   A) 1, 4, 9, 13, 15, 18, 21, 23, 26, 29
   B) 2, 5, 7, 10, 12, 16, 19, 22, 25, 28
   C) 3, 6, 8, 11, 14, 17, 20, 24, 27, 30

UNIT 1 Adjectives

🗝 ❶ **Comparatives**…比較級 ❷ **Superlatives**…最上級

LISTEN & READ

Keiko is showing a family photo to her boyfriend, John.

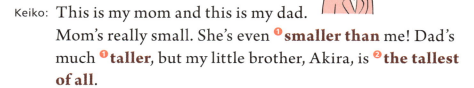

Keiko: This is my mom and this is my dad. Mom's really small. She's even ❶**smaller than** me! Dad's much ❶**taller**, but my little brother, Akira, is ❷**the tallest of all**.

John: What a beautiful photo! Who took it?

Keiko: My uncle Susumu. He's crazy about photography. Just the other day he bought a new digital camera. It was ❷**the most expensive camera** in the store!

John: Wow! He must be loaded! What's he like?

Keiko: He's so kind. I think he's ❷**the kindest uncle** in the world!

NOTES

- ☐ **smaller than ~**　（比較級の表現）〜より小さい
- ☐ **even smaller than ~**　さらに〜よりも小さい
  ※ than の後に me を用いるのは最近の傾向。本来は主語との比較なので、smaller than I となるところ。
- ☐ **the most expensive**　（最上級の表現）もっとも値段が高い〜
- ☐ **the kindest uncle**　（同じく）もっとも優しい叔父

形容詞

TRANSLATION

恵子はボーイフレンドのジョンに家族の写真を見せています。

Keiko: こちらが母で、こちらが父よ。母は小柄なの。私よりも小さいのよ。父はずっと背が高いけれど、弟のアキラが一番ノッポなの。

John: きれいな写真だね。どなたが撮ったの。

Keiko: 進おじさんよ。おじは写真が大好きなの。つい先日新しいデジカメを買ったのよ。お店で一番高いものをね。

John: へえ！　おじさんはお金持ちなんだね。彼はどんな人なの？

Keiko: とても優しいのよ。世界で一番優しいおじだと思うわ。

WORDS & EXPRESSIONS

- □ **uncle**　名 叔父・伯父　参 **aunt**　叔母・伯母
- □ **be crazy about ~**　～に夢中、～が大好き
  - 例 He's crazy about photography.
- □ **just the other day ...**　つい先日　参 **just** は強調
- □ **loaded**　形 お金持ちの、裕福な　類 **rich / wealthy**
- □ **What's he like?**　人柄などを尋ねる疑問文　参 **like** ~ は「～のような」

EXPLORING GRAMMAR

同じものを比べる

My salary is twice as much as yours.
私の給料は君の２倍です
✗ My salary is twice as much as you.

The shoes at this store are more expensive than those at that store.
この店の靴はあの店のものより値段が高い
☛ 靴が複数なので、それに合わせて that ではなく those を用いる。

比較級は２つのものを、最上級は３つ以上のものを比較する

Mt. Fuji is the highest mountain in Japan. 最上級
= **Mt. Fuji is higher than any other mountain in Japan.** 比較級
富士山は（他の一つ一つの）どの山と比べても高い

● 次の文はコミュニケーションでもよく間違える表現。

My brother is the faster of the two swimmers. 2人の比較
兄は２人のスイマーの中で速い方です
☛ the をつけることも注意。

My brother is the fastest of all the swimmers. 3人以上
兄はすべてのスイマーの中で一番速い

fewer と less を間違えない

● fewer は可算名詞に、less は不可算名詞に使う。
(few-fewer-fewest, little-less-least と変化する)

I have fewer books than my brother.
兄より持っている本の数が少ない
✗ less books

But my brother has less money.
しかし兄の方がお金が少ない

✗ fewer money

長い単語（3音節以上）には er, est ではなく more, most をつけて比較級、最上級にする

Elsa is more beautiful than Anna.

☛ 映画 "Frozen"『アナと雪の女王』ではアナがエルサに You are beautifuller.（あなたの方がきれいよ）という場面がある。すぐに I mean "You are more beautiful." と言い直している。文法的には間違いだが、最近の米語ではよく耳にする。

例外として、同じ人の2つの性質を比べる場合には、短い単語（2音節以内）でも more をつける。

My mother is more kind than strict to us.
母は厳しいというよりむしろ優しい

比較級、最上級を強める表現に注意

Dick is cleverer than Ben.
↓
強調すると……

Dick is much / far cleverer than Ben.
ディックはベンよりはるかに利口だ

✗ **Dick is very cleverer than Ben.**

☛ very で比較級を強調することはできない。

Jane is the tallest student in her class.
↓
強調すると……

Jane is much / by far the tallest student in her class.
ジェーンはクラスで断然一番背が高い

than ではなく to を用いる比較がある

- ラテン比較と呼ばれる prefer、senior、superior には than ではなく to を用いる。

I prefer coffee to tea.
= I like coffee better than tea.
紅茶よりもコーヒーが好きです

This camera is superior to that one.
このカメラの方があのカメラより優れている
反 **inferior**　劣っている

My cousin is three years senior to me.
=My cousin is three years older than I (am).
いとこは私より3歳年上です

Strategies for the TOEIC

• **Choose the correct word or words in brackets ( ).**

Can you remember...?

1. My cousin is three years senior (than / to) me.
2. My mother is (more kind / kinder) than strict to us.
3. Dick is (very / far) cleverer than Ben.
4. This camera is superior (than / to) that one.
5. I have (less / fewer) books than my brother.
6. My salary is twice as much as (yours / you).

Can you guess...?

7. My colleague is (junior / younger) to me by two years.
8. My son is the (harder / hardest) worker in his class.
9. Your thesis is very good, but Ben's has (fewer / less) mistakes.
10. Anna is the (more / most) intelligent of my two sisters.

Answers

1. to   2. more kind   3. far   4. to   5. fewer   6. yours
7. junior   8. hardest   9. fewer   10. more

UNIT 2 Adverbs of frequency & Articles

🗝 ❸ **Adverbs of frequency** … 頻度を表す副詞
❹ **Articles** … 冠詞

LISTEN & READ

Kate and Maki are university students (Kate is from San Francisco, USA). They meet in class for the first time.

Kate: Tell me Maki. What do you like doing at the weekends?

Maki: I love to go shopping! ❸**I often go shopping** with my sister. ❸**We usually get up** at six on ❹**a Saturday** to get ready for ❹**a whole day's shopping**!

Kate: Wow! ❸**I never get up** before seven at the weekends. But, as they say, ❹**"The early bird catches the worm!"**

Maki: Do you like to go shopping in ❹**the United States**, Kate?

Kate: Oh, sure, ❹**once or twice a month**. I guess I'm not ❹**a shopaholic** like you!

NOTES

☐ **often**　頻度を表す副詞「しばしば」、他の副詞も覚えよう。
　類 **frequently**　頻繁に　≒ **often**

☐ **go ~ing**　～しに行く
　※"目的の場所に行って～をする"場合は、go to ~ よりも go ~ing ＋場所が用いられる。
　　go swimming, go bowling, go skiing, go fishing など。

☐ **get up**　起きる　参 **go to bed**　床につく　　**sleep**　眠る
　例 **The early bird catches the worm.**　朝早く起きる鳥は虫を捕まえる（諺）
　　※ worm　ミミズなど　　insect　昆虫　　bug　コガネムシなど

頻度を表す副詞と冠詞

TRANSLATION

ケイトと麻紀は大学生です（ケイトはアメリカ、サンフランシスコ出身）。クラスで初めて会います。

Kate: ねえ、麻紀、週末に何をするのが好き？

Maki: ショッピング大好き！　お姉さんとよく買い物に行くの。丸1日の買い物のためにたいてい土曜日は6時に起きるの。

Kate: すごいわね。週末に7時前に起きることなんてないわ。でも「早起きは三文の得」って言うわね。

Maki: アメリカでも買い物に行くのが好き？

Kate: ええ、もちろん、月に1、2回ね。あなたのように買物中毒ではないけどね。

WORDS & EXPRESSIONS

- **at the weekends**　週末に　同 = **on weekends**
- **on a Saturday**　（不特定の）土曜日に
- **a whole day's shopping**　丸1日の買い物
- **as they say…**　…と（人が）言うように
- **I guess…**　…と思う　同 = **I think**
- **shopaholic**　名 買物中毒　類 **workaholic**　仕事中毒
    ※いずれも alcoholic addiction「アルコール中毒」からの造語

EXPLORING GRAMMAR

頻度を表す副詞

never 決して〜ない　　**sometimes** 時々
usually 普段は　　　　**frequently** 頻繁に　類 **often**
once in a while たまに　**every now and then** 時折
always いつも

否定に見えない副詞

(!) 見た目に否定に見えない副詞に注意しよう。

● rarely / seldom / hardly いずれも「めったに〜ない」という否定を表す副詞。

I like going to New York, but I rarely / seldom go downtown.
ニューヨークに行くのは好きだが、ダウンタウンにはめったに行かない

Not having met each other for a long time, I could hardly recognize my cousin at the airport.
お互い長い間会っていなかったので、空港でいとこがほとんど分らなかった

hard と hardly を区別

● 一般に形容詞に ly をつけると副詞になるので、hardly が hard の副詞形ではないかという誤解が生じる。
参 **hard** 副 一生懸命、熱心に　　**hardly** 否定の副詞

She is a kind nurse. 彼女は親切な看護師だ

She helped me kindly. 彼女は親切に手助けしてくれた

In this area it hardly rains in September.
この地域では9月にはほとんど雨が降りません

ly のつく副詞に注意

late 副 遅れて、遅く

Our professor always comes to class late.
私たちの教授はいつも授業に遅れてくる

● lately となると「最近」となり recently と同様の意味になる。

Have you heard from him lately / recently?
最近彼から便りがありましたか

The late mayor used to be against building a nuclear power plant in his city.
故市長は彼の市に原発を建設することに反対だった。
☛ late（形）を人につけると「亡くなった」ことになるので注意。

● most と mostly にも気をつけよう。

Sue is a most beautiful woman.
スーはとても美しい女性だ

Our dog is mostly asleep during the day.
うちの犬は昼間大抵寝ている

☛ この most は beautiful を強めているだけなので、the をつけない。the をつけると「もっとも美しい」となる。mostly は「大抵は」という意味。

always

- 頻度を表す副詞の中では最も使用頻度が高く「いつも」を表す。

  He is always on time. 彼はいつも時間厳守だ

  You are always a child in the eyes of your parents.
  親から見れば君はいつまでも子供だよ

- always が現在進行形とともに使われると「常習的行為」を表す。

  My boss is always finding fault with his staff.
  ボスは何かというと部下のあらさがしをしている

気をつけたい副詞

- already と yet：already は「もう」という意味であるが、疑問文に用いると「すでに完了の驚き」を表す。

  Have you eaten lunch already? It is still 11 o'clock.
  もうお昼を食べたの。まだ11時だよ

  この場合「驚き」を表しているので、**already** を用いてよいが、

  普通は……
  ↓

  Have you finished your assignment yet?
  もう課題は終わらせたの

  No, I haven't done it yet. いいえまだです

  のように、疑問文と否定文には **yet** を使うことに気をつけよう。

- ago と before：いずれも数詞の後につけ「〜前に」を意味するが、使い方の基本に注意。

- ～ago は現在を基準にするので、three days ago は「3日前」となり、過去時制で用いる。

    I came across this book at the auction site three days ago.
    この本は3日前に偶然オークションサイトで見つけたんだ

- before は過去を基準にして、その～前を表すので、過去完了時制と一緒に用いる。

    Both he and she could recognize each other. He had met her a few weeks before.
    彼も彼女もお互いに相手が分った。彼は（その）2、3週間前に彼女に会っていた

定冠詞

- the United States のように複数形の国名には the をつける。

    the Netherlands　オランダ

    the Republic of the Philippines　フィリピン

- 定冠詞を必要とする固有名詞：海、川、群島、山脈、砂漠など

    the Pacific　太平洋　　**the Sahara**　サハラ砂漠

    the Nile　ナイル川　　**the Alps**　アルプス山脈

- 普通名詞を抽象名詞として使うときも the を用いる。

    The pen is mightier than the sword.　文は武よりも強し

    When she saw the orphan, the mother rose in her heart.
    孤児を見たとき、彼女の心に母性愛が湧き起こった
    参 **the mother**　母性愛

形容詞に the をつけて、複数の人々を表す

The old (= Old people) are likely to be forgetful.
老人は物忘れしがちだ
☛ 動詞も複数に一致する。

We should be kind to the poor and the disadvantaged.
貧しい人や恵まれない人々に優しくすべきだ

Strategies for the TOEIC

• **Choose the correct word or words in brackets ( ).**

Can you remember...?

1. I often go (to shop / shopping) with my sister.
2. I like to go to New York, but I (rarely / don't rarely) go downtown.
3. She is a (kindly / kind) nurse.
4. Our professor always comes to class (late / lately).
5. My boss (is always / always is) finding fault with his staff.

Can you guess...?

6. (The Shinano / Shinano) is the longest river in Japan.
7. The attendees were (most / mostly) women in their thirties.
8. Have you turned in your essay (yet / already)? The deadline isn't until next month!
9. "Have you seen Jane (late / lately)?" "No, I haven't seen much of her."
10. I hardly (ever / never) travel by air.

Answers

1. shopping 2. rarely 3. kind 4. late 5. is always
6. The Shinano 7. mostly 8. already 9. lately 10. ever

UNIT 3 Auxiliary verbs

🔑 ❺ **be/have/do** … be 動詞／助動詞 have ／助動詞 do
　❻ **dare/used** … 助動詞 dare ／used

LISTEN & READ

Trevor and Angela Brown are tourists from the UK. They are on a trip to Japan with their kids Emily (16) and Georgie (12). They're in the hotel lobby.

Georgie: Dad, ❺**do** we **have to** carry our luggage to the room ourselves?

Trevor: No, Georgie. The porter will do it for us. He said ❺we **are to wait** for him till he comes.

Angela: You know, your dad ❻**used to work** part-time in a hotel in London. That's where we first met.

Emily: Really? I didn't know that. How did you meet?

Trevor: Well, your mom was such a rude guest and…

Angela: ❻**How dare you say** I was rude, Trevor! The truth is, the TV was broken so I complained, politely.

Trevor: That's right. And I went to repair it and it was love at first sight!

NOTES

☐ **Do we have to ~?**　～しなくてはいけないか？　≡ **Must we~?**

☐ **We are to wait for him…**　彼を待つように
※〈be 動詞＋to 不定詞〉で、「義務」「予定」「軽い命令」「可能」などの意味を表す。

☐ **He used to work…**　昔（以前）…で働いていた
※過去の習慣・状態を表す。

助動詞

TRANSLATION

トレバー、アンジェラ・ブラウンはイギリスからの旅行者です。
子供のエミリー（16歳）とジョージー（12歳）とともに日本を旅行中です。
彼らはホテルのロビーにいます。

Georgie: お父さん、荷物は自分たちで部屋まで運ばなくてはいけないの？

Trevor: いやいやジョージー。ポーターがやってくれるよ。来るまで待つように彼が言ったんだよ。

Angela: いいこと、お父さんは昔ロンドンのホテルでアルバイトしてたのよ。そのホテルで私たちは初めて出会ったのよ。

Emily: 本当？　そんなこと知らなかったわ。どんなふうに会ったの？

Trevor: そうだね、お母さんはとても失礼なお客さんでね……。

Angela: よくも私が失礼なんて言えるわね、あなた。本当はテレビが故障してたので、クレームを言ったのよ、丁寧にね。

Trevor: その通りだね。そこで父さんが修理に行って、ひと目ぼれしたんだ。

□ **That's where we first met.** where は関係副詞で、先行詞 the place などが省略されていると考える。
※「そこが (That) が私たちが初めて会った場所 (the place where)」と考える。従って That's where my brother works part-time. は、「あれが兄がバイトしているところです」となる。

□ **How dare you ~?** dare は助動詞で「あえて〜する」、How で始まる疑問文では「よくも〜できるわね」と不快・不満を表す慣用表現になる。
例 How dare you ask me for money?　よくも私にお金の無心ができるね

WORDS & EXPRESSIONS

- □ **luggage** 名荷物（英）　同 = **baggage**（米）
- □ **part-time** 副形パートで、パートの
- □ **rude** 形失礼な、無礼な
- □ **guest** 名ホテルなどの客
  ※お店の客は customer、乗客は passenger、弁護士や会計士などの顧客は client、病院にかかるのは patient。区別して使おう。
- □ **the truth is** 本当のところは
- □ **complain** 動不平を言う、クレームをする　参英語の **claim** は「要求する」
- □ **politely** 副丁寧に、形 **polite** ↔ **rude**
- □ **repair** 動修理する、口語では fix も使える。
- □ **It was love at first sight.** （いわゆる）一目ぼれだった

EXPLORING GRAMMAR

Do we have to ~

- 「～しなくてはいけないですか」
  have to ～は「～しなくてはいけない」で must とほぼ同じ意味で使える。

"Do we have to carry our luggage to our room ourselves?"
手荷物は自分たちで部屋に運ばなくてはいけないですか

> これに対する返事は……
> ↓

"Yes, you / we have to." 必要です／ **"No, you / we don't have to." or "No, you / we need not."** その必要はありません

他の「義務」などを表す助動詞

- ought to / should は "主語のするべき義務" を表す。

You should / ought to submit your assignment by 17:00 next Monday.
来週の月曜日の 17:00 までに課題を提出するべきです

☛ must や have to と異なり、"常識や良心からの義務" と考えるのが自然。いずれもまだその「動作が遂行されていない」ニュアンスを伴う。たとえば、I should / ought to drive safely, because we are near an elementary school. 「小学校の近くだから、気をつけて運転するべきだ」の場合はそれまでは「あまり気をつけていなかった」し、ひょっとすると「その気はないかも」ととれる。「その気があるなら」I must / have to drive safely. とすると行為が遂行される可能性が高まる。また、must は "話し手の課する義務" を表す。have to は "周囲の状況から課される義務" と考える。

This is a Chinese dish of my wife's own cooking, so you must try some.
妻のお手製の中華料理だから、少しは食べてもらわないと

☛ 話者の考え・気持を表している。

You have to keep quiet during the concert.
コンサートの間は静かにしなくてはいけない
☛ 誰もが守らなくてはいけない義務。

had better は「した方がいい」ではない

☛ 中学・高校の授業で上のような意味で教わった人も多いと思うが、had better は「優しく勧めている」のではなく、「その行為が遂行されないと来るであろう事態も含めて強く強いる」表現である。従って must / have to → had better → should / ought to が強さの順である。had better が上記の意味を持つと「脅し」にまで発展することもあるので、注意が必要。

You must / have to keep to the left in England.
イギリスでは左側通行をしなくてはいけない

You had better tell me the truth. Otherwise I'll …
本当のことを話しなさい。さもないと……

You should / ought to keep your promise.　約束は守るべきです

〈be 動詞＋to 不定詞〉の表す意味

● 予定

We are to leave for London by plane.
飛行機でロンドンに発つ予定です

● 義務

As long as you're a student, you are to obey school regulations.
学生である限り、学則には従うべきだ

- 可能

    Not a footstep was to be seen on the snow.
    雪の上には足跡は一つも見られなかった

- 軽い命令

    I'll take care of this work, so you are to get ready to go out.
    私はこの仕事をかたづけるから、君は出かける準備をしなさい

    You are to send me a reply e-mail right away.
    すぐに返信メールを送ってね

used to と would

- used to は「昔 (以前) 〜したものだ」と「継続的にしていた」ことを表現する。

    When I was a student, I used to study in the library till late.
    学生時代は図書館で遅くまで勉強したものだ

    My father used to take a walk in the morning.
    父は朝散歩したものだ

- これに対して、would は「(継続的ではないが) 頻繁にしていた」ことを表す。

    When I was late for the class, my teacher would make me stand in the corner of the classroom.
    私が授業に遅刻すると、先生は私を教室の隅に立たせたものでした

    I would often sing to his guitar.
    よく彼のギターに合わせて歌ったものでした

    ☛ often など頻度を表す副詞とともに使われる。

● 「昔の状態を表す」場合は used to だけが使える。

There used to be a pond in the garden.
昔、庭に池がありました

dare

● 疑問文と否定文の中では助動詞として使われる。

How dare he use my phone without my permission!
彼はよくも許可なく私の電話を使うわね
☞ Dialogue の中でも How dare の形で使われているが、この文型が多い。

He dared not run for the city mayor.
彼はあえて市長選には出馬しなかった

Strategies for the TOEIC

• **Choose the correct word or words in brackets ( ).**

Can you remember...?

1. Not a footstep was (to be seen / to see) on the snow.
2. You (should / ought) to submit your assignment by 17:00 next Monday.
3. You (have / had) better tell me the truth.
4. (Have / Do / Are) we have to carry our luggage to our room ourselves?
5. You (may / must / have) to keep silent during the concert.

Can you guess...?

6. Do passengers (should / have to) wear a seatbelt?
7. (Why / How / Who) dare you speak to me like that!
8. He left strict instructions. We (aren't / don't) to wait for him.
9. When I was young, we (used / use) to listen to records, not CDs.
10. I think you (should / must / ought) to apologize for your rude behavior.

Answers

1. to be seen 2. ought 3. had 4. Do 5. have 6. have to 7. How 8. aren't 9. used 10. ought

UNIT 4 Conditionals (1)

❼ Zero conditional … 条件文（０型）
❽ First conditional … 条件文（１型）

LISTEN & READ

Keiko and John are discussing their plans for the summer vacation.

John: Keiko, ❼**do you mind if we travel** somewhere in Japan this summer? I have to finish an important project at work.

Keiko: Oh, John! You promised we would visit Italy this year. ❽**If you finish** your project early, **will you be** able to take some time off?

John: Well, ❼**provided I finish** all my work, **I guess we can go** for a few days.

Keiko: Oh, please, John! ❽**If you take** me to Italy, **I promise I won't spend** all your hard-earned money on clothes and accessories!

John: Well, that's a relief!

NOTES

□ 〈**do you mind if** S + V〉　～ではどうですか
　※ mind は「～を気にする」が元の意味なので、もし「いいよ」と言いたいときは "No, not at all."「もちろんいいよ」（いいえ、全く気にしません）となる。うっかり "Yes." と答えると、「はい、嫌です」となるので、気をつけよう。

参 〈**provided** S + V〉は〈**if** S + V〉の formal な言い方。

条件文 (1)

TRANSLATION

恵子とジョンは夏休みの計画について話し合っています。

John: 恵子、この夏は日本のどこかに旅行に行くのはどうだい。重要なプロジェクトを完成しなくてはいけないんだ。

Keiko: まあ、ジョン！ 今年はイタリアに行くって約束したじゃない。早めにプロジェクトが終わったら、少しは休みがとれるんでしょう？

John: そうだね、仕事が全部終わったら、2、3日出かけられると思うよ。

Keiko: まあ、お願い、ジョン！ イタリアに連れていってくれるなら、あなたの稼いだお金を全部衣服やアクセサリーに使ったりしないって約束するわ。

John: ああ、それを聞いて安心したよ。

WORDS & EXPRESSIONS

- mind　動 気にする
- take time off　休みをとる　参 take a day off　1日休む
- I guess…　…と思う　同 ＝ I think
- not ~ all…　全部〜というわけではない　部分否定
- hard-earned　形 一生懸命稼いだ
- That's a relief!　それを聞いて安心したよ　同 ＝ I'm relieved to hear that.

EXPLORING GRAMMAR

条件文0型 & 1型

- ☛ 0型は特に「条件」を表すのではなく、「…したら～」〈Do you mind if S＋V?〉などが良い例。本文にある、Provided I finish all my work, I guess we can go for a few days. も「仕事が全部終われば、2、3日は出かけられると思うよ」と自分の都合を述べている。

● **条件文1型は「単なる条件」を表す。**
  - ☛ 文法規則として、"時と条件を表す副詞節では、単純未来は現在形で表記する"を覚えておこう。

If you run to the station, you will catch the train.
駅まで走れば、電車に間に合うでしょう
  - ☛ If you run の部分が条件を表す副詞節。内容は "これから走る" ので、走るのが未来でも "現在形" で表す。主節の you will catch は未来形で表す。you can catch と "可能" を表す助動詞を用いることもできる。

The dog will bite you if you pull her ear.
耳をひっぱったらその犬は噛むよ
  - ☛ if の節が後にくる構文もある。

● **不変の真実を述べる場合などは、主節も現在形を用いる。**

If you boil water, it turns to vapor.
水は沸騰すると水蒸気になる

● **次の文を考えてみよう。**

If you will attend the ceremony, I would really appreciate it.
もしあなたが式典に出てくだされば、本当にありがたいのですが
  - ☛ この文では If 節の中で will を用いているが、この場合は "意志未来" で "厚意" を表すので will を用いる例外と考えよう。

● 他のいくつかの例を見てみよう。

If it continues to rain hard, the plane will not take off on schedule.
豪雨が続けば飛行機は予定通りに飛ばないだろう

If you want to lose weight, you should refrain from eating so much rice.
減量したいなら、ご飯をそんなに食べるのは控えるべきです
　☛ 同じ意味を、If you want to lose weight, eat less rice. と命令文で言うこともできる。

If you have finished writing your essay, you had better submit it before you forget it.
エッセイを書き終えてしまったんだったら、忘れないうちに提出しなさい

のように、現在完了形を用いることもある。また、

If you are waiting for the No. 10 bus, you will have to wait for another half an hour.
１０番バスを待っているのなら、あと３０分待たなくてはいけませんよ

のように If 節に現在進行形を用いることもある。

STRATEGIES FOR THE TOEIC

• **Choose the correct word or words in brackets ( ).**

CAN YOU REMEMBER...?

1. (Provide/ Provided) I finish all my work, I guess we can go for a few days.
2. Do you mind if we (will travel / are going to / travel) somewhere in Japan?
3. The dog (will bite / would bite / bites) you if you pull her ear.
4. If it (is continuing / continued / continues) to rain hard, the plane will not take off on schedule.
5. If you (want / wanted) to lose weight, (eat / eating) less rice.

CAN YOU GUESS...?

6. If you don't eat your ice cream, it (would melt / melts / will melt).
7. When I get home late, my mom (will get / gets / is getting) angry.
8. If you (arrive / will arrive) late for class, you (will be / are) in big trouble!
9. Do you mind if I (am smoking / smoke / will smoke)?
10. I (will sit / sit) here, if you don't mind.

Answers

1 Provided **2** travel **3** will bite **4** continues **5** want, eat
6 will melt **7** gets **8** arrive, will be **9** smoke **10** will sit

UNIT 5 Conditionals (2)

- ❾ Second conditional … 条件文（2型）
- ❿ Third conditional … 条件文（3型）

LISTEN & READ

Kate and Maki are talking about Kate's mother's birthday.

Kate: I wonder what I should do for my mom's birthday. ❾**If I had** enough money, **I could visit** her in San Francisco.

Maki: I had no idea it was your mom's birthday! ❿**If I'd known, I would have bought** a little something for her this morning in the city.

Kate: What a kind thought, Maki. I know. ❾**If we were to video-call** her, **she'd be thrilled!**

Maki: But my cheap PC doesn't have a camera. ❿**Had I bought** the more expensive model, **we could have video-called** her.

Kate: Not to worry! Let's go to the internet café down the road. We can call her from there! After all, it's the thought that counts, isn't it?

NOTES

☐ **If I had enough money, I could visit…**
　もしお金があれば、訪ねることができるのに　仮定法過去形

参 **If I had known, I would have bought…**
　もし知っていたとしたら、…買っただろうに　仮定法過去完了形

条件文 (2)

TRANSLATION

ケイトと麻紀はケイトのお母さんの誕生日のことを話しています。

Kate: お母さんの誕生日をどうしようかしら。もしお金が十分にあれば、サンフランシスコに会いに行けるんだけど。

Maki: あなたのお母さんの誕生日のことをまったく知らなかったわ。もし知っていれば今朝、街でちょっとしたものを買ったのに。

Kate: まあ、優しいのね、麻紀。そうね、もしビデオ電話でもできれば、お母さんはきっと感激するわね。

Maki: でも私のしょぼいパソコンにはカメラがついてないわ。高い方のモデルを買っていれば、あなたのお母さんにビデオ電話できたのに。

Kate: 心配いらないわ。この先のインターネットカフェに行きましょう。そこからなら電話できるわよ。結局、大切なのは気持ちよね。

WORDS & EXPRESSIONS

- □ **wonder +** Ⓥ 参〈I wonder ＋疑問詞〉で「〜かしら」という意味
- □ **I had no idea…**　…をまったく知らなかった
- □ **a little something**　ちょっとしたもの・気の利いたもの
- □ **What a kind thought!**　直訳すると、「なんて優しい考えね・優しいのね」くらい
- □ **video-call**　動ビデオ通話［コール］、カメラを取りつけたパソコンでインターネット回線を利用して、お互いの顔を見ながら通話すること
- □ **be thrilled**　動（大）感激する
- □ **Not to worry.**　心配いらないよ　同＝ Don't worry.
- □ **internet café**　ネットカフェ
- □ **down the road**　この（通りの）先の
- □ **count**　動大切である
  例 **It is the thought that counts.**　大切なのは気持ちだ

EXPLORING GRAMMAR

> 仮定法を学ぼう

☛ 〈If S ＋過去形、助動詞の過去形＋動詞の原形〉の構文：条件文2型は "仮定法過去形" と呼ばれる。現在の事実に反する仮定を表す。例えば、As I don't have enough money, I can't buy this dress.「お金が足りないのでこのドレスが買えない」ことが事実である。これを If I had enough money, I could buy this dress.「お金が十分にあれば、このドレスが買えるのに」と表現するのが仮定法過去形。"事実に反する仮定" を表すのに、動詞 have を過去形の had にして、主節には過去形の助動詞 could を使う。

● 〈I wish＋S＋過去形〉：
「〜であればよいのに」という現在の思いを表現する。

I wish I were as rich as you.
君のように裕福であればいいのに

事実は……
↓
I am sorry I am not so (as) rich as you.
君のように裕福でないことが残念だ

I wish I could run as fast as you.
君のように速く走れればいいのに

これも事実は……
↓
I am sorry I can't run so (as) fast as you.
君のように速く走れないのが残念だ

- 〈If S＋過去完了形、助動詞の過去形＋have＋過去分詞〉：
条件文3型は"仮定法過去完了形"と呼ばれ、過去の事実に反する仮定を表す。

If I had met him before, I could have recognized him at the airport.
前に彼に会っていれば、空港で彼が分かっただろうに
☛ 初めて会ったので、空港で認識できなかったことを述べている。

事実は……
↓
As I had not met him before, I could not recognize him at the airport.

- 〈I wish＋S＋過去完了形〉：
「～であったらよかったのに」と過去の願望を表現する。

I wish I had studied harder when I was young.
若いころにもっと勉強しておけばよかったのに

実際は……
↓
I am sorry I didn't study hard when I was young.
若いころに熱心に勉強しなかったことが残念だ

では、**I am sorry you didn't attend the ceremony.** を仮定法で言い換えると、

I wish you had attended the ceremony.
君がその式典に参加していたらなあ

と過去のことを残念がる表現になる。

仮定法の慣用表現

- If it were not for ~　もし~がなければ
"現在の事実に反する仮定"。

If it were not for his age, we could hire him right now.
彼の年齢のことさえなければ、今すぐ彼を雇うことができるのに

If it were not for air, no animal could live.
空気がなければ、動物は生きられないだろう
☛ 主節は〈助動詞の過去形＋動詞の原形〉となる。

- If it had not been for ~　もし~が（過去に）なかったら
"過去の事実に反する仮定"。主節は〈助動詞の過去形＋have＋過去分詞〉。

If it had not been for his rescue, we could not have survived.
彼の救助がなかったら、私たちは生き延びられなかっただろう

If it had not been for the bottled water, the victims might have died.
ボトルに入った水がなければ、被害者は死んでいたかもしれない

- But for ~ , Without ~　もし~がなければ、なかったならば
現在と過去のいずれの事実に反する仮定にも使える表現。

But for / Without his assistance, we could not succeed in the new project.
= If it were not for his assistance, we could not succeed in the new project.
彼の援助がなければ、新しいプロジェクトはうまくいかないだろう

過去のことに用いると……
↓
But for / Without my deceased parents' estate, I could not have set up my company.
両親の遺産がなければ、会社は設立できなかっただろう

となる。

これも言い換えると……
↓
If it had not been for my deceased parents' estate, I could not have set up my company.

となる。

- ⟨If S + were to ~⟩「万が一~ならば」と可能性のほとんどない未来のことを仮定するときに用いる。主節は⟨助動詞の過去形＋動詞の原形⟩。

If I were to make a space journey, I would go to Venus.
もし宇宙旅行をするなんてことがあれば、火星に行くだろう

If he were to make a marriage proposal to me, I would accept it with pleasure.
万が一彼がプロポーズしてくれるなら、喜んで受けるのに

Strategies for the TOEIC

Can you remember...?

- **Choose the correct word or words in brackets ( ).**

1. If I (have / had) enough money, I could buy this dress.
2. I wish I (could / can) run as fast as you.
3. If I (had / have) met him before, I (could recognize / could have recognized) him at the station.
4. If it (has / had) not been for the bottled water, the victims might (die / have died).
5. I wish I (am / would be / were) as rich as you.
6. I wish you (attended / had attended / were attending) the ceremony.

Can you guess...?

- **Fill the blanks with the correct form of the verbs in brackets ( ).**

7. If I _____ you were married, I wouldn't have proposed! (know)
8. I didn't have a cold. If I _____ a cold, I certainly wouldn't have gone to the party. (have)

- **Choose the correct word or words in brackets ( ).**

9. I (wish / hope) I (can / could) fly!
10. If you (study / have studied / studied) harder, you would be more popular with the girls.

Answers

1 had **2** could **3** had, could have recognized **4** had, have died
5 were **6** had attended **7** had known **8** had had (I'd had)
9 wish, could **10** studied

UNIT 6 Conjunctions

⑪ Contrastive conjunctions
… 接続詞：等位接続詞／従属接続詞

LISTEN & READ

The Browns are visiting Shinjuku.
Trevor is having trouble following his map.

Trevor: Mm. We seem to be lost.
I don't know where we are
⑪ **even though** I did my best to follow this map.

Angela: Maps are useful. ⑪ **However**, the best way to navigate a place like Shinjuku is by using a smartphone. Here, look!

Emily: Cool, Mom! Now we know exactly where we are. *Ka-bu-ki…* what?

Trevor: Kabukichou! Yes, we know where we are now, ⑪ **but** it's not where we wanted to go. This is the seedy part of town!

Georgie/Emily: Cool!

NOTES

- ⟨**even though** + ⟩　たとえ〜でも
- **However**　しかしながら
    ※この場合は But を用いても同じ意味を伝えられる。いずれも "対比接続詞" と呼ばれる。

接続詞

TRANSLATION

ブラウン一家は新宿を訪れています。
トレバーは地図で道を探すのに苦労しています。

Trevor: ウム。どうやら迷ったようだ。この地図に従って一生懸命やったんだけどどこにいるのかわからない。

Angela: 地図は役に立つわ。でも、新宿のようなところで道順を探すのは、スマホを使うのが一番よ。ほら、見て。

Emily: すごいわ、ママ。これでどこにいるか正確にわかるわね。カブキ…何ですって？

Trevor: 歌舞伎町だって！　そうだね、今どこにいるのかわかったね、でも行きたいところとは違うね。ここは評判の良くないところだよ。

Georgie/Emily: いけてるじゃん。

WORDS & EXPRESSIONS

- **do one's best** 最善をつくす
- **useful** 形 役に立つ・有効な
- **navigate** 動 道順を教える・指示する
- **smartphone** 名 スマホ
- **exactly** 副 正確に・正しく
- **seedy** 形 怪しげな・評判の悪い
- **Cool!** すごい！・カッコいい

EXPLORING GRAMMAR

接続詞の確認：2種類の接続詞

● 等位接続詞：

and, but, both… and, or, either… or, neither… nor, not only …but also

などがある "名詞・形容詞・副詞・動詞・句・節を対等の関係で" 接続する。

My father is a teacher and scholar.
父は教師であり、研究者でもある
☛ 一人で兼任と考えるので冠詞 a は teacher と scholar の両方にかかる。

He sometimes publishes books but he never makes a speech.
時々本を出しますが、講演はしません

He makes his study both at college and at home.
研究は大学と自宅の両方でします

He will teach either in Japan or in the States next year.
来年度は日本か合衆国のどちらかで教えます

He is not only a prestigious professor but also a respectable father.
彼は高名な教授であるだけでなく、尊敬できる父親です

● 従属接続詞：

if, that, though, although, when, unless, as, since

など、名詞節や副詞節を結びつける。等位接続詞との分かりやすい違いは、2つ（以上）の節を2文に分けると文が成り立たないことである。
He works hard, but he makes little money. は **He works hard. But he makes little money.** としても文は成り立つが、**If he makes haste, he will be in time.** は **If he makes haste. He will be in time.** は第一文が不自然になる。

Rumor has it that they got married.
噂によると彼らは結婚したそうだ

Though/Although he graduated from graduate school, he couldn't find a good job.
彼は大学院を卒業したのだけれど、良い仕事に就けなかった

When he got to the station, the last train had already left.
彼が駅に着いたときには最終列車はすでに出てしまっていた

Many of us didn't take to the newcomer, because she was often putting on airs.
私たちの多くは新入生を好きになれなかった、というのも彼女はよくお高くとまっていたからだ

Unless you make an effort, you will not pass the exam.
努力しないと試験に受からないよ
　☛ unless は if ... not と同意。

● 理由を表す接続詞：

as, since, because

などがある。

As / Because / Since he is honest, he is looked up to by everyone around him.
彼は正直なので周りのだれからも尊敬されている

● 時を表す接続詞：

when, while, as

などがある。

He had a hard time making himself understood in English when (while) he was in London.
彼はロンドンにいる間、英語が通じなくて苦労した

接続詞の用法、注意事項

- either A or B「A か B のどちらか」、neither A nor B「A も B も～ない」が主語になる構文では動詞（の数）は B に合わせる：

Either his teacher or his classmates are expected to attend the meeting.
彼の先生か、クラスメートのどちらかが（どちらもが）その会議に出ることが望まれている

Neither my father nor my brothers were in the wrong.
父も兄たちも間違ってはいなかった

☞ どちらの文も動詞は後の his classmates, my brothers に合わせて are, were を用いる。

- both A and B「A も B も両方」は A と B の両方が主語となるので常に複数扱いである：

Both you and I are to blame. 君も僕も悪いんだ

参 **be to blame** 〈be 動詞＋to 不定詞〉は既習「責められるべき」→「悪い」

in spite of~（前置詞句）、despite~（前置詞）はそれぞれ「～にもかかわらず」という意味であるが、後に名詞を伴うので接続詞ではない。

In spite of / Despite his repeated requests, the publishing company turned down his suggestions.
彼のたび重なる要望にもかかわらず、その出版社は彼の提案を断った

この文を接続詞を使って表現すると……
↓
Although / Though he requested repeatedly, the publishing company turned down his suggestions.

となる。

Strategies for the TOEIC

Can you remember...?

- **Choose the correct word or words in brackets ( ).**

1. He will teach (both / either) in Japan or in the States next year.
2. (Though / But / Not only) he graduated from graduate school, he couldn't find a good job.
3. (If / When) he got to the station, the last train had already left.
4. (Although / Unless) you make an effort, you will not pass the exam.
5. He had a hard time making himself understood in English (in spite of / while / during) he was in London.
6. (Despite / In spite) of his repeated requests, the publishing company (turned down / didn't turn down) his suggestions.

Can you guess...?

- **Choose the best conjunction to fill each blank.**

  but / unless / however / even though

7. I understand your problem, Mr. Jones. _____, I'm afraid I can't help you.
8. I love fish, _____ I don't like it raw.
9. _____ I studied hard, I still failed the test.
10. _____ you tidy your room, you can't go out tonight!

Answers

1. either 2. Though 3. When 4. Unless 5. while 6. In spite, turned down 7. However 8. but 9. Even though 10. Unless

UNIT 7 *Future forms*

⑫ **shall, will, present continuous, be going to**…未来を表す

LISTEN & READ

*Kate and Maki are preparing for a university test.
They are at their apartment.*

Kate: The telephone's ringing.
⑫**Shall I answer it?**

Maki: It's OK. ⑫**I'll get it.** Hello.

Ken: Hi! Maki. It's me, Ken. ⑫**I'm coming** to Tokyo tomorrow for a few days.

Maki: Oh, hi, Ken. That's great! But ⑫**we're going to have** a test tomorrow, so **we can't see** you until the day after.

Ken: That's cool. I can wait.

Maki: By the way, where ⑫**are you staying?**

Ken: **I'm staying** at the Imperial Palace Hotel in Ikebukuro. Anyway, ⑫**I'll call** again tomorrow evening. Good luck with your test!

NOTES

☐ **Shall I ~?**　〜しましょうか（相手の意思を聞く表現）

☐ **I'll get it.**　私が出ます　参 その場で決めた未来は **will** を使って表す。

☐ **I'm coming to Tokyo.**　東京にいる麻紀が主体となるので、「そこに行く」を表すのに come を用いる。進行形で「近い未来」を表す。
　参**Where are you staying?**　同じく「滞在予定」という未来を表す。

未来形

TRANSLATION

ケイトと麻紀は大学の試験の準備をしています。彼らはアパートにいます。

Kate: 電話が鳴っているわ。出ましょうか？
Maki: いいわ。私が出る。もしもし。
Ken: やあ、麻紀。健だよ。2、3日の予定で明日東京に行くんだよ。
Maki: こんにちは、健。それはいいわね。でも明日試験があるのよ、だから明後日まで会えないわ。
Ken: 大丈夫。待てるよ。
Maki: ところで、どこに泊まるの？
Ken: 池袋のインペリアルパレスホテルだよ。明日の夜もう一度電話するよ。試験頑張ってね。

WORDS & EXPRESSIONS

- **ring** 動 (電話などが) 鳴る
  参 **I'll give you a ring.** 電話するわ or 指輪をあげる
- **answer** 動 (電話) に出る、ノックにこたえる
- **the day after** 明後日 同 = the day after tomorrow
- **That's cool.** それは素晴らしい・いいね 参 **He's cool.** 彼はかっこいい
- **by the way** ところで (話題を変えるときに用いる) 同 = incidentally
- **Good luck!** 幸運を祈る・頑張ってね
  参 舞台などに出る人には "**Break a leg!**" とも言う、これも「頑張ってね」である。

EXPLORING GRAMMAR

未来を表す表現

will と be going to は「同じ」と中学・高校では教えているようだが、実はかなり用法が違う。興味のある人は、『実例英文法』(A.J.トムソン／A.V.マイティネット著、オックスフォード出版、p.279) を参照されたい。

will も be going to も「意図」(〜するつもり) を表すが、be going to は「常にあらかじめ考えられた意図」、will は「意図」のみを表し、前もって考えていたものでないことが普通。準備までしてきたことには be going to を用いるのが正しい。

I bought a new digital camera and I'm going to take many photos of my family.
新しいデジカメを買ったので、家族の写真をたくさん撮るつもりだ

☛ ここで will を用いると、強勢を置かない限り (強く読まないと) 意図が強く感じられない。電話が鳴ったり、ドアをノックする音が聞こえた場合には、(あらかじめ準備はないので) will を用いなければならない。

There is a knock on the door. ノックだわ

OK. I'll go and see who it is. 誰だか見に行くわ

その他の「あらかじめ」かどうか不明の場合はいずれを用いても OK。

I will / am going to buy a new house someday.
いつか新築の家を買うつもりだ

天気は"確実な予想"はできないものの一つであるが、

The sky is overcast. It's going to rain at any moment.
空が (急に) 暗くなってきたわ。今にも降りそうね

これはかなり確実と思われるので、**be going to** を用いると切迫した感が強い。**It will rain.** だと確実性が弱い。

I will always follow you. いつでもあなたについていきます

など「強い意志」を表すときには **will** に強勢を置いてその意志を表す。

● be going to を用いなくても現在進行形で「近い未来」を表すことができる。

未来を表す副詞を伴うことが多いが、状況から未来が分かる場合は問題なく使える。高校で教わったと思うが、動詞には往来発着を表すものが用いられる、**come, leave, bring**（連れてくる、持ってくる）、**take**（連れていく、持っていく）、**arrive, fly**（飛行機で行く、来る）、**start, drive**（車で行く、来る）や **die** なども含まれる。

"Why are you dying, Mama?" "It's my time, Forrest. Death is just a part of life."
「お母さんどうして死ぬの？」「フォーレスト、私の番なんだよ。死も人生の一部にすぎないんだよ」（映画、*Forrest Gump* より）

When are you leaving for London?
いつロンドンに発つのですか

I'll be seeing you.　また近いうちに会いましょう

という慣用表現もある。

We're taking an exam in September.　9月には試験があります

相手の意志を尋ねる表現

● Shall I ～？は相手の意志を尋ね、Shall we ～？は自分も含めた意志を尋ねる。

I'm sorry but our manager is on another phone. Shall I have him call you back?
申し訳ありませんが、部長は別の電話に出ています。後で折り返し電話をさせましょうか

Shall we take a short rest, since we have been working since morning?
朝から働きづめなので、少し休憩をとりましょうか

同意する場合は "**Yes, let's.**"（はいそうしましょう）、同意しないなら、"**No, let's not.**"（いいえ、やめましょう）となる。少し高度になるが、"**Shall he come for you?**" と3人称に **shall** を使うと「彼にあなたを迎えに行かせましょうか」と第三者に何かを「～させましょうか」という意味になる。

この場合の返事は……
↓
Yes, let him come for me.
はい、彼に迎えに来させてください

などと表現する。

Strategies for the TOEIC

- **Choose the correct word or words in brackets ( ).**

Can you remember...?

1. The sky is overcast. It's (raining / going to rain) at any moment.
2. I bought a new digital camera and (I'll / I'm going to) take many photos of my family.
3. Why (will you die / are you dying), Mama?
4. (We shall take / We're taking) an exam in September.
5. The telephone's ringing. (Shall / Will) I answer it?

Can you guess...?

6. (I'm going to get married / I'm getting married) in three days.
7. It's such a lovely day. I think (I'm going / I'll go) to the park.
8. (I'm going to visit / I'm visiting) my grandmother this afternoon, but don't tell her. It's a surprise!
9. Don't worry, it (isn't snowing / won't snow) tomorrow.
10. Of course I love you, and (I'm going to / I will) always love you!

Answers

1. going to rain 2. I'm going to 3. are you dying 4. We're taking
5. Shall 6. I'm getting married 7. I'll go 8. I'm going to visit
9. won't snow 10. I will

UNIT 8 Verbs (1)

🗝 ⑬ **Gerund**…動名詞   ⑭ **Infinitive**…不定詞

LISTEN & READ

Trevor and Angela are enjoying looking at the sunset from the balcony of their hotel in Okinawa.

Trevor: Just look at that sunset, kids! Have you ever seen anything like it?

Angela: Yes! ⑬ **Seeing is believing!**

Emily: Mm. It's no big deal! I'd rather watch TV.

Trevor: I guess ⑬ **there's no accounting for taste!**

Angela: She's just a child, Trevor. When she's older, ⑬ **she'll enjoy looking** at beautiful sunsets, just like we do!

Trevor: Well, ⑭ **I intend to make** the most of this trip. ⑭ **I refuse to waste** a single, precious moment!

Georgie: Ha, ha! You really ⑬ **love winding dad up**, don't you, Emily?

NOTES

- **Seeing is believing!**　百聞は一見にしかず（諺）To see is to believe. とも。
  ※"見ることは信じることになる"から「見なくては分からない」とも。

- **It's no big deal!**　大したことない　同＝ **It's not a big thing.**
  参 "No bones broken."　大したことない
  ※怪我などを心配されたときに用いる。

- **I'd rather…**　（…に動詞の原形を入れて）むしろ…したい 慣用表現

- **There's no accounting for taste.**
  ※文字通りの意味は"好み (tastes) は説明できない"諺の「蓼食う虫も好き好き」に当たる
  参 **account for**　〜を説明する 句動詞

動詞 (1)

TRANSLATION

トレバーとアンジェラは沖縄のホテルのバルコニーから夕日を見て楽しんでいます。

Trevor: 子供たち！ ほら、あの夕日を見てごらん。こんなにきれいなものを見たことがあるかい。

Angela: すごいわ！「百聞は一見にしかず」ね。

Emily: んー！ 大したことないわ。テレビを見る方がいいわ。

Trevor: 「蓼食う虫も好き好き」だね。

Angela: まだ子供なのよ、あなた。大人になれば、私たちのようにきれいな夕陽を楽しんで見るわよ。

Trevor: やれやれ、僕はこの旅行を最大限に楽しむつもりさ。一瞬もこの貴重な時を無駄にするのはお断りだね。

Georgie: ハハ！ エミリーはパパを焚きつけるのが好きなんだから、そうだね、エミリー？

WORDS & EXPRESSIONS

- **sunset** 名 夕日
- **intend** 動 〜するつもりである
- **refuse** 動 拒否する 同 = **turn down**
- **waste** 動 無駄にする
- **precious** 形 貴重な
- **wind (＋人＋) up** さまざまな意味があるが「たきつける」「怒らせる」「挑発する」など。

Exploring Grammar

動詞の後にさらに動作をつけ加える形に動詞の ~ing 形と to~ 形がある。それぞれを使い分けられるように身につけよう。

動名詞だけを目的語にとる動詞

deny, avoid, miss, mind, enjoy, give up, abandon, finish, escape, postpone, stop, put off（アルファベット順でないのは頭文字による覚え方のため）ここに挙げた動詞は目的語としてとる動詞は ~ing 形になる。

Do you mind waiting for me at the front desk?
フロントで待ってくれますか

We should avoid getting into trouble.
いざこざに巻き込まれないようにするべきだ

Due to the storm we had to postpone (=put off) leaving for the summit.
嵐のために頂上に向けての出発を延期しなくてはいけなかった

Have you finished writing your thesis yet?
もう論文は書き終えましたか

不定詞だけを目的語にとる動詞

intend~　〜つもりだ　　　**refuse~**　〜を拒否する
learn~　〜習い覚える　　　**manage~**　どうにか〜する
offer~　〜を申し出る　　　**promise~**　〜することを約束する
tend~　〜する傾向がある　　**agree~**　〜することに同意する

● 主に否定文で

bother~　わざわざ〜する　　**afford~**　〜する余裕がある

● 否定や疑問文で

care to~　〜したい

- **seem ~**　～に思える　　**appear ~**　～に見える

などは It を主語にして書き換えることもできる

She seems to be diligent.　彼女は勤勉そうだ
参 It seems that she is diligent.

He appeared to be hiding something.
彼は何かを隠しているように見えた
参 It appeared that he was hiding something.

I can't afford to study abroad.　留学する余裕はない

My father didn't bother to drop by my office.
父はわざわざ会社に寄ってくれることはしなかった

My teacher tends to criticize the present political situation.
私の先生は現在の政治情勢を批判しがちだ

We are going to throw a potluck party this coming Friday. Do you care to come?
今度の金曜日に持ち寄りパーティーをやるんだけど。来たいですか

目的語に不定詞をとるか動名詞をとるかで意味が変わる動詞

- **forget, remember**

I forgot to send this letter on my way to my office.
会社に行く途中でこの手紙を出すのを忘れた

☛ この文ではまだ手紙を投函していない。"to ~" の場合は "実施していない動作" を表す。"~ ing" を取る場合はその動作を "実施したことを忘れる" という意味になる。反対の意味を表す remember の方がわかりやすい。

Please remember to turn off the air-conditioner when you leave the room.
部屋を出るときにはエアコンを切ることを覚えておいてね

☛ この場合 "これからする動作" を表している。"Don't forget to turn off ~" と言っても同じ意味になる。

動名詞を用いて……

I remember meeting him once, but I don't remember where.
彼に一度会ったことは覚えているが、どこで会ったのか覚えていない

と言うと、"会った" という動作を覚えていることを表している。

- regret

    I regret having made such a mistake.
    そのようなミスをしたことを後悔している

    ☛ "過ぎたこと" を表すので、having ＋過去分詞を用いている。それに対して、I regret to say that Ms. Sato's lecture has been canceled. と to 不定詞を用いると「残念ながら、佐藤先生の講義は休講となりました」と "これから述べること" を申し訳なく思っていることを表す。この意味では to say, to tell, to inform など「伝える」動詞を伴う。

- stop

    I stopped smoking.　禁煙した

    The man stopped to smoke.
    その男は煙草を吸うために立ち止まった

    ☛ to smoke は "目的" を表す不定詞の副詞的用法

- like

    一般的に **like** は to 不定詞、動名詞のいずれも目的語としてとれるが、多少ニュアンスが異なる。

    I like playing baseball.　野球をするのが（一般的に）好き

    But today I would like to play tennis.　でも今日はテニスをしたい

    と個別的に述べる場合は **would like to ~** の形をとる。

- mean

    mean to ~　～するつもりである　　≡ **intend to ~**

I didn't mean to hurt your feelings.
君の感情を害するつもりはなかったんだ

mean ~ing　〜することになる・〜することを意味する

Missing the last train means having to take a taxi home.
終電を逃すとタクシーで帰宅することになる

● **try**

try to~ は「〜しようと（努力）する」に対して **try ~ing** は「試しにしてみる」と伝わる意味が異なる。

I tried to persuade him, only to fail.
彼を説得しようとしたが、（結局）ダメだった

He tried sending an e-mail to Susan to convey his feelings, but she didn't reply.
気持ちを伝えようと彼はスーザンにメールを送ってみたが、彼女からの返信はなかった

● **go ~ ing**

その場所に行って行動をする慣用表現。

go skiing　スキーに行く　　**go camping**　キャンプに行く
go fishing　釣りに行く　　**go boating**　舟に乗りに行く
go shopping　買い物に行く　**go bowling**　ボーリングに行く
go hunting　狩りに行く　　など。

I went fishing in Lake Hamana with my family.
家族と浜名湖に釣りに行った

☞ 浜名湖に行ってから釣りをするので、I went fishing to Lake Hamana としない。

買い物も同じように……
↓

My mother and I went shopping at the department store yesterday.
昨日、母と私はデパートに買い物に行った

動名詞だけをとる要注意の慣用表現

- look forward to ～ ing　～するのを楽しみにしている

  I'm looking forward to hearing from you.
  あなたからの便りを楽しみにしています

  What do you say to ~ing?　～するのはどうですか
  I'll have a day off next week. What do you say to going to the zoo?
  来週1日休めるけど、動物園に行くのはどうですか

- be worth ～ ing　～する価値がある

  Kyoto is worth paying a visit to.
  京都は訪れる価値がある

  This book is not worth reading.　この本は読む値打ちがない

- be used / accustomed to ～ ing　～するのに慣れている

  Are you used to eating fish raw?
  お魚を生で食べるのに慣れていますか

  He is accustomed to speaking in public, because he is a statesman.
  彼は政治家だから、人前で話すのに慣れている

- when it comes to ～ ing　～するとなると、～する段になると

  I'm all thumbs when it comes to making something by myself.
  自分で何かを作るとなると、全く不器用なのです

  When it comes to speaking in public, I feel nervous.
  人前で話すとなると、緊張します

Strategies for the TOEIC

Can you remember…?

- **Choose the correct word or words in brackets ( ).**

1. Have you finished (to write / writing) your thesis yet?
2. I can't afford (to study / studying) abroad.
3. Please remember (to turn / turning) off the air-conditioner when you leave the room.
4. I remember (to meet / meeting) him once, but I don't remember where.
5. I regret (to say / saying) that Ms. Sato's lecture has been cancelled.
6. I went (to fish / fishing) in Lake Hamana with my family.
7. When it comes to (speak / speaking) in public, I feel nervous.

Can you guess…?

- **Fill the blanks with a form of the word 'use'.**

8. I didn't mean _____ your pen. I thought it was mine.
9. I'm still not accustomed _____ chopsticks.
10. I'm looking forward _____ my new electronic dictionary.

Answers

1. writing 2. to study 3. to turn 4. meeting 5. to say
6. fishing 7. speaking 8. to use 9. to using 10. to using

UNIT 9 Look

🗝 ⑮ **Look + adjective** 〈sound/feel/smell + 形容詞〉
Look + like + noun 〈sound/feel/smell + like + 名詞〉
「〜に見える／聞こえる／感じる／におう」
⑯ **Look + clause**…〈look + 節 (S + V)〉「〜に見える」

LISTEN & READ

John is leaving for work, but Keiko is worried.

Keiko: You ⑮**look pale**, John. Are you feeling alright?

John: I ⑮**feel lethargic**, but I'm OK. Just a little under the weather.

Keiko: You ⑯**look as if you're catching a cold.** And ⑯**it looks as though it's going to snow today,** so why don't you call in sick?

John: Keiko, you ⑮**sound like my mother!** Don't worry, I'll be fine. What's that you're cooking?

Keiko: It's tonight's dinner.

John: Mm. ⑮**Smells good!** I'm looking forward to it when I get home.

Keiko: Now you ⑮**sound just like my father!**

NOTES

☐ **be under the weather** 体調が悪い
※もとは、「舟に乗っていて→海が荒れて→揺れて酔い→気分が悪くなる」ことから
反 **be in the pink** 元気である
 My wife is always in the pink. 妻はいつも元気いっぱいだ
参 **She is in pink.** ピンクを着ている

☐ **Why don't you 〜?** 〜してはどうですか ※誘う文
同 = How about calling in sick?

～に見える

TRANSLATION

ジョンは仕事に出かけるところだが、恵子は心配しています。

Keiko: ジョン、顔色が悪いわよ。大丈夫？

John: だるいんだよ、でも大丈夫。ちょっと気分が悪いだけだよ。

Keiko: 風邪をひきかけているように見えるわ。それに、今日は雪が降るみたいだし、今日は「病欠」ってことで電話したら？

John: 恵子、母さんみたいに言うなよ。心配いらないよ、良くなるから。何を料理してたの？

Keiko: 今夜の食事よ。

John: んー。いいにおいだ。家に戻ったら楽しみだね。

Keiko: いやだ、お父さんみたい。

WORDS & EXPRESSIONS

- **pale** 形 顔色が悪い
- **alright** 大丈夫 同 = all right
- **lethargic** 形 気力がない・だるい
- **call in sick** 病気で休むと電話する
- **look forward to + Ⓥ** ～を楽しみにする
  参 Ⓥ（目的語）が動詞の場合は ~ing 形にする。 ➡ Unit 8 参照

EXPLORING GRAMMAR

look の用法

- 〈S＋look＋形容詞〉 ～に見える
  この形容詞は補語（C）。

  You look stunning in that wedding dress.
  そのウェディングドレス姿、すてきだよ

  You look under the weather. 気分が良くないようだね
  ☛ このように look の後に Idiom（熟語）がくることもある。

- 〈S＋look like＋名詞〉 ～のように見える

  You look like a million bucks today.
  今日は見違えるように魅力的だね

  look like の後に人間以外が来ることもある……
  ↓
  It looks like rain. 雨が降りそうだ

  また、そう言った人に……
  ↓
  Well, it looks like it. エー、そのようですね

  と答えることもできる。

  That boat looks like a dot from far away.
  遠くから見るとあの船も点のように小さく見える

  Don't look like that. そんな顔をするなよ
  ☛ look like の後に〈S＋V〉が来ることもある。この場合 Dialogue にある、〈It looks as if / as though＋S＋V〉と同じような意味を表す。

  (It) Looks like life's been treating you well.
  素敵な人生を送られているようですね

- ⟨look as if / as though S＋V⟩（この場合は条件文2型）

It looks as if you're going to propose to me.
まるで私にプロポーズするつもりみたいね

look に関しての注意点

She looked calm when she heard the news.
彼女はその知らせを聞いたとき落ち着いていた
☛ calm は"補語"。

言い換えると **She had a calm expression when she heard the news.** となる。次の文を見てみよう。

The coach looked calmly at the excited players yelling at each other.
監督は、興奮してお互いにののしり合っている選手を落ち着いて見ていた
☛ この calmly は looked を修飾する副詞。

You're looking good, this morning!
今朝はすてきだね
☛ 現在進行形にして"今"を強調することもある。

sound の用法

- look が「～に見える」に対して、sound は「～に聞こえる、～と響く」となる。

The potluck party you suggested sounds great.
君が提案した持ち寄りパーティーは良さそうだね

His idea sounds interesting.　　彼の考えは面白そうだ

☛ この2文は⟨S＋sound＋形容詞⟩の構文。look の場合と同じくこの形容詞は補語（C）。

- ⟨S ＋ sound like ＋ 名詞⟩　～のように聞こえる
  この構文も look と同様に考える。

  What you said sounds like a dream come true.
  君の言ったことは願ったりかなったりだね

  You always sound like my mother.
  あなたはいつも母みたいな話し方ね

  Because you always sound like a broken record.
  だって同じことばかり繰り返すんだから
  ☛ look と同じく、as if / as though の構文でも使える。

  You sound as if / as though you're going to turn in your letter of resignation.
  辞表を提出しそうな口ぶりだね

smell の用法

- look、sound と使い方は同様。

  This beefsteak smells very good.
  このステーキはおいしそうなにおいです

  That meat smelled like a goat.　あの肉は臭かった

  Your drink smells like a mixture of juice and beer.
  君の飲み物はジュースとビールを混ぜたもののようなにおいだ

Strategies for the TOEIC

Can you remember...?

• **Choose the correct word or words in brackets ( ).**

1. You (look/ look like / look as if) stunning in that wedding dress.
2. It looks (as though / like) rain.
3. You (look as if / look like / look) under the weather.
4. It (looks / looks as if) you're going to propose to me.
5. (Looks / Looks like) life's been treating you well.
6. What you said sounds (as if / like) a dream come true.

Can you guess...?

• **Fill the blanks with the correct forms of 'look', 'sound' or 'smell'.**

7. Mm. That roast chicken _____ delicious!
8. Well, from what you say, it _____ you had a great time!
9. Nice picture! Your boyfriend _____ a movie star!
10. Stop complaining. You _____ my mother.

Answers

1. look 2. like 3. look 4. looks as if 5. Looks like 6. like
7. looks / smells 8. sounds as if / sounds as though 9. looks like
10. sound like

UNIT 10 Modal verbs (1)

- ⑰ **Obligation (present/future)** … 義務（現在／未来）
- ⑱ **Obligation (past)** … 義務（過去）

LISTEN & READ

Maki and Kate are talking about a research trip to Kyoto and Maki's university assignments.

Maki: I really want to go on the research trip to Kyoto this year. ⑰**Must I sign up** for it now?

Kate: No, ⑰**you don't have to.** But ⑰**you ought to finish** all your assignments before then.

Maki: Mm. ⑰**I still have to finish** my essay on Hemmingway.

Kate: Haven't you finished it yet? You know, ⑱**you should have turned it in** last Friday. That was the deadline.

Maki: Really? Oh, no! ⑱**I really should have known better** than to put it off.

Kate: ⑰**You ought to ask** Professor Sato for an extension. She's very kind. I'm sure she'll give you more time.

NOTES

- ☐ **Must I ~?** の返事として、「いいえ、その必要はありません」の場合は、**No, you don't have to.** または **No, you need not.** が自然。
  "義務"を表す **ought to** は **should** との言い換えが可能。

- ☐ **turn in** は目的語が代名詞の場合は **turn it in** のように動詞と副詞 **in** の間に置く。普通名詞の場合は **turn the essay in** でも **turn in the essay** でも良い。

- ☐ **know better than to ~** ～しなくても良いくらいの分別がある
  参 **I should have known better than to ~** ～してしまってバカだった

助動詞 (1)

TRANSLATION

麻紀とケイトは京都への研究調査旅行と麻紀の大学での課題について話しています。

Maki: 今年は本当に京都に研究調査に行きたいの。今申し込まないといけないの？

Kate: いいえ、その必要はないわよ。でも、その前に課題をすべてこなすべきよ。

Maki: うん。まだヘミングウェイのレポートを完成しなくてはいけないのよ。

Kate: まだ終わっていないの？　いいこと、先週の金曜日までに提出するべきだったのよ。それが締め切りだったのよ。

Maki: 本当？　まさか？　バカだわ、延期しなくてはいけないなんて。

Kate: 佐藤教授に締め切りを延期してもらうようお願いするべきだわ。彼女はとても優しいから、きっと時間をくださると思うわ。

WORDS & EXPRESSIONS

- ☐ **research trip** 名 研究調査のための旅行
- ☐ **assignment** 名 課題
- ☐ **essay** 名 （文化系科目の）レポート、エッセイ
- ☐ **(Ernest) Hemmingway** ヘミングウェイ (1899–1961)
- ☐ **You know,** いいこと、ねえ
- ☐ **turn in** ～を提出する
- ☐ **deadline** 名 締め切り
- ☐ **put off** 延期する
  ※目的語が代名詞の場合は、put it off となることに注意。turn it in も思い出そう。
- ☐ **extension** 名 延長
- ☐ **sign up for sth** ～に申し込む・登録する　同 = **register (for)**~

Exploring Grammar

義務を表す must

I am exhausted, so I must get some rest.
ひどく疲れているので、休まなくてはいけない

Must I see the doctor right away? Yes, you must.
すぐにお医者さんに診てもらわなくてはいけませんか？　はい、そうです

No, you don't have to. / No, you need not.
いいえその必要はありません

☛ ここで、No, you must not. と言うと「いいえ、そうしてはいけません」と"禁止"を表す。

● must には語形変化がないので、過去時制、未来時制、完了形では have to に言い換える。

I didn't have a fever, so I didn't have to go to the hospital.
熱はなかったので、病院に行く必要はなかった

All the doors being locked, the fire fighters had to break down some of them.
ドアにはすべて鍵が掛かっていたので、消防士はドアをいくつか壊さなくてはいけなかった

☛ この場合は実際に「壊した」ことも含む。

If you want to study abroad in the future, you will have to study English more.
将来留学したいのなら、英語をもっと勉強しなくてはいけないでしょう

義務を表す ought to / should

- must や have to よりは"義務感"が弱いがそれでも「～すべきだ」と義務を表す。

If you want to lose weight, you ought to / should get more exercise.
痩せたいなら、もっと運動をするべきだ

- 否定文の場合は not の位置に気をつけること

The boarding students ought not to / should not go out of the dorm late at night.
寮生たちは夜遅く外出すべきではない

☛ ought to には過去形がないので、間接話法では形が変わらない。

He said I ought to / should attend the conference the next day.
彼は私が翌日の会議に出席するべきだと言った

また疑問文では……ought と to が離れる。
↓
Ought I to / should I know who the tutor is?
家庭教師が誰だか知るべきでしょうか

〈助動詞＋have＋過去分詞〉で過去の義務などを表す

You should have prepared for the exam much earlier.
君はもっと早めに試験の準備をするべきだったのに（"しなかったこと"を責めている）

☛ この場合も ought to で言い換えられる。

I ought to have thought much of her feelings.
彼女の気持ちをよく考えるべきだったのに（"しなかったこと"を後悔している）

> この2文のように1人称（I）の場合は「後悔」、2・3人称（you・he など）の場合は「責める」気持ちが表現される。

He should have arrived at the ceremony on time.
彼は式典には時間通りに到着するべきだったのに（"間に合わなかった"ことを責めている）

● must の場合は"義務"ではなく、"断定"を表す。

Somebody must have amended his thesis, for it is almost error free.
誰かが彼の論文に修正を加えたに違いない、というのもミスがほとんどないからだ

同 = **I'm sure somebody has amended his thesis.**

参 "義務"であれば must have + 過去分詞ではなく、**had to** を使う。

He had to resign owing to his mistakes.
彼は失敗のために辞職せざるを得なかった

> 〈need not + have + 過去分詞〉の場合は、"する必要のないことをした"ことを表す。

We need not have hurried to the station, because the train was delayed.
電車が遅れていたので、駅まで急ぐ必要はなかった（のに急いでしまった）

You need not have watered the flowers in the garden. It began to rain.
お花に水やりをするには及ばなかった。雨が降り始めました

Strategies for the TOEIC

Can you remember...?

• **Choose the correct word or words in brackets ( ).**

1. I didn't have a fever, so I (mustn't / didn't have to) go to the hospital.
2. If you want to study abroad in the future, you will (must / have to) study English more.
3. I am exhausted, so I (must to / must) get some rest.
4. (Have to / Must) I see the doctor right away?
5. Ought I (know / to know) who the tutor is?
6. Should I (know / to know) who the tutor is?
7. You should (had prepared / have prepared / prepared) for the exam much earlier.
8. Somebody (should have / must have) amended his thesis, for it is almost error free.

Can you guess...?

• **Fill the blanks with a form of 'have to'.**

9. Yesterday, I _____ apologize for my selfish behavior. My mom says I _____ be more careful in the future.
10. Do I _____ wear this stupid uniform? I never _____ wear one before.

Answers

1. didn't have to 2. have to 3. must 4. Must 5. to know
6. know 7. have prepared 8. must have 9. had to, have to
10. have to, had to

Review 1

Fill the blanks. Use the words in brackets ( ) to help you.
If the words are separated by a slash (/), choose the correct word or words.

🔑 Grammar Keys ❶ ~ ❻

A. This is my mom and this is my dad. Mom's really small. She's even _____ (small) me!

B. Dad's much _____ (tall), but my little brother, Akira, is _____ (tall) of all.

C. I love to go shopping! I _____ go shopping with my sister. We _____ get up at six on _____ Saturday to get ready for _____ whole day's shopping! (a / often / never / usually / the / ever)

D. Dad, _____ we _____ (have to) carry our luggage to the room ourselves?

E. You know, your dad _____ (used / use) to work part-time in a hotel in London.

🔑 Grammar Keys ❼ ~ ❿

F. Keiko, do you mind if we _____ (travel) somewhere in Japan this summer?

G. If you _____ (finish) your project early, _____ you _____ (be able to) take some time off?

H. If I _____ (have) enough money, I _____ (can visit) her in San Francisco. But unfortunately I don't, so I can't.

I. I had no idea it was your mom's birthday! If I _____ (know), I _____ (buy) a little something for her this morning in the city.

J. We seem to be lost. I don't know where we are _____ (even if / even so / even though) I did my best to follow this map.

K. The telephone's ringing. _____ (Will / Shall / Do) I answer it?

L. I _____ (come) to Tokyo tomorrow for a few days. I've already booked a hotel.

🗝 Grammar Keys ⓭ ~ ⓲

M. When she's older, she'll enjoy _____ (look) at beautiful sunsets, just like we do!

N. I intend _____ (make the most of) this trip. I refuse _____ (waste) a single, precious moment!

O. I _____ (feel like / feel as though / feel) lethargic, but I'm OK. Just a little under the weather.

Review 1

P. You _____ you're catching a cold. And it _____ it's going to snow today, so why don't you call in sick? (look / look as if / looks as though / looks)

Q. You ought _____ (finish) all your assignments before you go on the research trip.

R. Haven't you finished it, yet? You know, you should _____ it _____ (turn in) last Friday. That was the deadline.

Answer Key

A. She's even <u>smaller than</u> me!

B. Dad's much <u>taller</u>, but my little brother, Toby, is <u>the tallest</u> of all.

C. I <u>often (usually)</u> go shopping with my sister. We <u>usually (often)</u> get up at six on <u>a</u> Saturday to get ready for <u>a</u> whole day's shopping!

D. Dad, <u>do</u> we <u>have to</u> carry our luggage to the room ourselves?

E. You know, your dad <u>used</u> to work part-time in a hotel in London.

F. Keiko, do you mind if we <u>travel</u> somewhere in Japan this summer?

G. If you <u>finish</u> your project early, <u>will</u> you <u>be able to</u> take some time off?

H. If I <u>had</u> enough money, I <u>could visit</u> her in San Francisco.

I. If I <u>had known</u>, I <u>would have bought</u> a little something for her this morning in the city.

J. I don't know where we are <u>even though</u> I did my best to follow this map.

K. <u>Shall</u> I answer it?

L. I'<u>m coming</u> to Tokyo tomorrow for a few days.

M. When she's older, she'll enjoy <u>looking</u> at beautiful sunsets, just like we do!

N. I intend <u>to make the most of</u> this trip. I refuse <u>to waste</u> a single, precious moment!

O. I <u>feel</u> lethargic, but I'm OK.

P. You <u>look as if</u> you're catching a cold. And it <u>looks as though</u> it's going to snow today, so why don't you call in sick?

Q. You ought <u>to finish</u> all your assignments before you go on the research trip.

R. You know, you should <u>have turned</u> it <u>in</u> last Friday.

UNIT 11 Modal verbs (2)

⑲ Probability (present/future) … 断定（現在／未来）
⑳ Probability (past) … 断定（過去）

LISTEN & READ

The Browns are having dinner in their hotel restaurant, but Georgie isn't there.

Trevor: Is Georgie in the room?

Angela: Yes. I think ⑲**he must be sick.** He has such a small appetite.

Trevor: ⑲**He might be tired** after our trip to Okinawa.

Angela: Mm, ⑳**he must have picked something up** on the journey back.

Emily: Or ⑳**he might have got** food poisoning from the raw fish we had yesterday.

Angela: Or ⑲**it could be** just a bad cold.

Georgie: Hi, guys! What's for dinner? I'm starving!

Angela / Trevor / Emily: Huh?

NOTES

- **have a big / small appetite** 大いに食欲がある／ない
  例 **I have a small appetite.** 食欲があまりない
  ※ I have no appetite. 食欲がまったくない

- **I'm starving.** "近接未来" を表す表現で「飢え死にしそう」がもとの意味。
  ※言い換えとして、I could eat a horse. も、同様に空腹を表す。

助動詞 (2)

TRANSLATION

ブラウン一家はホテルのレストランで夕食のテーブルについていますが、ジョージーがいません。

Trevor: ジョージーは部屋にいるのかい。

Angela: そうよ。具合が悪いに違いないわ。食欲がないんですもの。

Trevor: 沖縄旅行の疲れかもしれないよ。

Angela: うーん、旅行から帰る途中で何か病気にかかったに違いないわ。

Emily: それとも、昨日食べた刺し身にあたったのかもしれないわ。

Angela: それとも、ただの悪い風邪かも。

Georgie: やあ、みんな！　夕食は何だい？　腹ペコだよ！

Angela/Trevor/Emily: はあ？

WORDS & EXPRESSIONS

- [ ] **sick** 形 具合が悪い
- [ ] **appetite** 名 食欲
- [ ] **pick (sth) up**　sth に感染する　※本来の「拾う」「手に入れる」の応用。
- [ ] **journey** 名 （乗り物を使った長めの）旅行
- [ ] **food poisoning** 名 食中毒・食あたり
- [ ] **raw fish** 名 生魚・刺し身

EXPLORING GRAMMAR

断定を表す表現（現在 & 過去）

- "推量"する気持ちは may, might「〜かもしれない」で表すが、その気持ちが"断定"となると must を用いる。

    You must be very tired after such a long flight.
    長い空の旅でさぞお疲れでしょう（とても疲れているに違いない）

- I'm sure you are very tired ... といい換えられる。これが過去についての断定となると、must＋have＋過去分詞で表す。

    He must have told a lie, because everything turned out false.
    彼は嘘をついたに違いない、というのもすべてが虚偽と判明したのだから

- これらの反対の意味"〜のはずがない"を表すには can't, cannot を用いる。

    He can't be hungry, because he has just eaten a large hamburger. 現在
    彼は大きなハンバーガーを食べたばかりだから、おなかがすいているはずがない

    He cannot have written the essay all by himself. It's too good. 過去
    彼がひとりでその論文を書いたはずがない、できすぎだ

- 少し"推量"の例文を挙げておこう。

    You look pale. You may be feverish. 現在
    顔色が悪いよ、熱があるかもしれないよ

    He ought to be here by this time. He may have missed the train. 過去
    彼は今ごろにはここに着いていてもいいはずだ。電車に乗り遅れたのかもしれない

- "推量"を表す場合に may の代わりに might を用いると「ひょっとしたら～かもしれない」という意味になる。

   Dialogue の **He might be tired after our trip to Okinawa.** は
   He may be tired... でも表せるが推量の度合いが少し変わる。

遠回しに推量を表す could

- **Dialogue** の It could be just a bad cold. の中の could は可能性から推量を遠回しに表現するときに用いられる。

   may, might でも推量は表せるが、**could** の方がさらに婉曲な表現。表すのは"現在の推量"である。

   A lot of wars could be prevented. 現在
   多くの戦争は（避けようと思えば）避けられるのかもしれない

   "What's wrong with you? You look under the weather."
   "Well, it could be a lot of things, but I can't tell why." 現在
   「どうしたの。元気がないようよ」
   「そうだね、いろいろ可能性が考えられるけど、なぜだかわからないんだ」

   "What makes you think that way?" "Well, I could be in the wrong, but I can't help thinking like this." 現在
   「どうしてそんなふうに考えるんだ」「そうですね（謙虚に）間違っているかもしれませんが、どうしてもそう思えるんです」

- 他の助動詞と同じように、"過去についての推量"は〈could ＋ have ＋ 過去分詞〉。

   The same thing could have happened to anybody. 過去
   同じことは誰に起きても不思議はなかった

Strategies for the TOEIC

Can you remember...?

• **Choose the correct word or words in brackets ( ).**

1. He must (tell / told / have told) a lie, because everything turned out false.
2. He (might / must / can't) be hungry, because he has just eaten a large hamburger.
3. You (can't / must) be very tired after such a long flight.
4. You look pale. You (may have been / may be) feverish.
5. He ought to be here by this time. He (may miss / may have missed) the train.
6. A lot of wars (could be prevented / could prevent).

Can you guess...?

• **Fill the blanks with forms of 'must', 'can't' or 'may/might'.**

7. Who's at the door? It _____ be Alex, she's in Spain.
8. Barry got straight A's! His parents _____ be delighted!
9. I'm not entirely sure, but I _____ left my keys in your car yesterday.
10. What? You're getting married? You _____ be serious!

Answers

1 have told **2** can't **3** must **4** may be **5** may have missed
6 could be prevented **7** can't **8** must **9** may have / might have
10 can't

UNIT 12 Nouns (1)

🔑 **㉑ Compound nouns & Acronyms** … 合成（複合）名詞＆頭文字

LISTEN & READ

Kate and Maki are having lunch on the university campus. Maki is looking at some photos on her smartphone.

Kate: Wow! Who's that? Is that your ㉑**boyfriend**?

Maki: I wish! No, he's a famous Japanese ㉑**movie star**.

Kate: Why do you have a picture of him on your ㉑**smartphone**? Do you like him?

Maki: I guess so. I took it last week at my dad's office.

Kate: Really? What does your dad do?

Maki: He's the ㉑**CEO** of a big advertising company and he often gets ㉑**VIPs** to advertise for his clients.

Kate: That's so cool! Can you take me one day?

Maki: Sure!

NOTES

- **I wish!**　そうだといいのだけど 仮定
  同 **I wish he were my boyfriend!**　彼がボーイフレンドだったらいいのだけれど
- **I took it.**　it は the picture / the photo のこと。
- **CEO**　Chief Executive Officer の頭文字で「最高経営責任者」。米国の多くの州では president も officer の一員とされている。
- **VIP**　🈳 Very Important Person の頭文字。
- **one day**　いつか・不特定のある日
  参 **some day** と同様に用いるが、**one day** は「過去のある日」も意味する点が違う。

名詞 (1)

TRANSLATION

ケイトと麻紀は大学のキャンパスでお昼を食べています。麻紀はスマホの写真を見ています。

Kate: あら！ それは誰？ ボーイフレンド？

Maki: だといいんだけど。違うの、日本の有名な映画俳優よ。

Kate: なぜ、スマホにその人の写真を入れているの？ 好きなの？

Maki: そうかもね。先週父の会社でその写真を撮ったの。

Kate: 本当？ お父さんは何をなさっているの？

Maki: 大きな広告会社の社長なの、だから広告の依頼者のために有名人を連れてくるの。

Kate: それはすてきね！ いつか私も連れて行ってくれる？

Maki: もちろんいいわよ！

WORDS & EXPRESSIONS

- ☐ **Wow!** ワー ※驚きを表す
- ☐ **I wish!** そうだといいのだけど
- ☐ **I guess so.** そうね、そうかもね ※Yes の代わりに遠回しに
- ☐ **What does (S) do?** 何をなさっているの？・職業は？
- ☐ **CEO** 名 同 = president 社長
- ☐ **advertising company** 名 広告会社
- ☐ **VIP** 名 重要人物・著名人
- ☐ **advertise** 動 宣伝する
- ☐ **client** 名 依頼人（この場合は「広告主」）
- ☐ **That's so cool!** それはすてきね 参 **cool** カッコいい
- ☐ **Sure!** （口語で）もちろん

EXPLORING GRAMMAR

合成名詞

本来 a beautiful flower のように名詞を修飾するのは形容詞であるが、名詞・動名詞が一緒になって意味を形成することがある。

● 〈名詞＋名詞〉の例

Tokyo Tower　東京タワー
gas station　ガソリンスタンド（イギリスでは petrol station）
kitchen sink　台所の流し台　　**rice cooker**　炊飯器
country roads　田舎道　　**June bride**　6月の花嫁
tennis court　テニスコート　　**department store**　百貨店
woman doctor　女医

● 〈動名詞＋名詞〉の例

dining table　ダイニングテーブル　　**waiting list**　補欠人名簿
driving license　運転免許証　　**sleeping car**　寝台車
parking lot　駐車場　　**reading glasses**　読書用老眼鏡

● 〈名詞＋動名詞〉の例

weight lifting　重量挙げ　　**bird watching**　野鳥観察
head- hunting　人材スカウト　　**problem-solving**　問題解決（の）

覚えておくと便利な acronym（頭文字語）など

ATM (automated teller machine)　現金自動預け払い機
AIDS (acquired immunodeficiency syndrome)　エイズ
APEC (Asia-Pacific Economic Cooperation Conference)
　アジア太平洋経済協力閣僚会議
ASEAN (Association of Southeast Asian Nations)
　東南アジア諸国連合
AV (audio-visual)　視聴覚
BS (broadcasting satellite)　放送衛星
B/S (balance sheet)　貸借対照表

CATV (cable television) 有線テレビ
CD (compact disc) コンパクトディスク
CIF (cost, insurance and freight) 運賃・保険料込み値段
COD (cash on delivery) 代金引換払い
COO (chief operating officer) 最高執行責任者
CS (communication satellite) 通信衛星
CPU (central processing unit) 中央演算処理装置
DH (designated hitter) 指名打者
DIY (do-it-yourself) 日曜大工
DWI (driving while intoxicated) 酔っぱらい運転
EU (European Union) 欧州連合
ETA (estimated time of arrival) 到着予定時間
EV (electric vehicle) 電気自動車
FBI (Federal Bureau of Investigation) 米連邦捜査局
FRB (Federal Reserve Bank) 連邦準備銀行
GATT (General Agreement on Tariffs and Trade)
　関税と貿易に関する一般協定
GDP (gross domestic product) 国内総生産
GNP (gross national product) 国民総生産
G7 (Conference of Ministers and Governors of the Group of Seven) 先進7カ国蔵相・中央銀行総裁会議
HIV (human immunodeficiency virus) ヒト免疫不全ウイルス
IAEA (International Atomic Energy Agency) 国際原子力機関
IC (identification card / integrated circuit)
　身分証明書／集積回路
ILO (International Labour Organization) 国際労働機関
IMF (International Monetary Fund) 国際通貨基金
IOC (International Olympic Committee) 国際オリンピック委員会
ISBN (International Standard Book Number) 国際標準図書番号
ISO (International Organization for Standardization)
　国際標準化機構
IWC (International Whale Committee) 国際捕鯨委員会
JAS (Japanese Agricultural Standards) 日本農林規格

LCD (liquid crystal display) 液晶ディスプレー
LED (light emitting diode) 発光ダイオード
M&A (merger & acquisition) 合併・買収
MBA (Master of Business Administration) 経営学修士
MC (master of ceremony) 司会者
NASA (National Aeronautics and Space Administration) 米国航空宇宙局
NATO (North Atlantic Treaty Organization) 北大西洋条約機構
NGO (non-governmental organization) 非政府(間)組織
ODA (Official Development Assistance) 政府開発援助
OECD (The Organization for Economic Cooperation and Development) 経済協力開発機構
OEM (original equipment manufacturing) 相手先ブランド生産
OPEC (Organization of Petroleum Exporting Countries) 石油輸出国機構
PAYE (pay-as-you-earn taxation) 源泉課税方式
PET (polyethylene terephthalate resin) ポリエチレン・テレフタレート樹脂
POS (point of sales [system]) 販売時点情報管理
PPM (parts per million) 100万分の1
RM (risk management) 危機管理
ROM (read only memory) 読み出し専用メモリー
SALT (Strategic Arms Limitation Talks) 戦略的兵器制限交渉
SDF (Self Defense Forces) 自衛隊(正式名は Japan Self-Defense Forces)
TOB (take-over bid) 株式公開買い付け
UFO (unidentified flying object) 未確認飛行物体
UNESCO (United Nations Educational, Scientific and Cultural Organization) ユネスコ
VAT (value added tax) 付加価値税
WHO (World Health Organization) 世界保健機関
ZEG (zero economic growth) 経済ゼロ成長

STRATEGIES FOR THE TOEIC

• Fill the blanks with words from this unit.

CAN YOU REMEMBER...?

1. In America, you can get gas at a _____.
2. On an overnight train journey, you can sleep in a _____.
3. A woman who gets married in June is sometimes called a _____.
4. You can park your car in a _____.
5. ATM stands for _____.
6. ASEAN stands for _____.
7. UNESCO stands for _____.

CAN YOU GUESS...?

8. You brush your teeth with a _____.
9. When you study abroad, you can stay with a family in their home. This is called a _____.
10. TOEIC stands for _____.

ANSWERS

1. gas station   2. sleeping car   3. June bride   4. parking lot (🇬🇧 car park)   5. automated teller machine   6. Association of Southeast Asian Nations   7. United Nations Educational, Scientific and Cultural Organization   8. toothbrush   9. homestay   10. Test Of English for International Communication

UNIT 13 Nouns (2)

㉒ **Countable and uncountable nouns**…可算名詞と不可算名詞

LISTEN & READ

Keiko and John have just moved into a new apartment. They're wondering how to spend the weekend.

Keiko: Why don't we go into town this weekend and buy some ㉒**furniture** for our new apartment? It looks so sad and bare.

John: That's a good idea, but I don't think it's much ㉒**fun** spending the weekend shopping for furniture. I know! Let's go somewhere!

Keiko: Really? I'd love to spend a couple of days at the beach.

John: OK. I'll make a ㉒**reservation** for a room at the Beach Front Hotel right away!

NOTES

☐ **furniture**　不可算名詞（数えられない名詞）
　参 **a piece of furniture**　1点の家具
　例 **a lot of / much furniture**　たくさんの家具
　　✗ many furnitures

☐ **fun**　不可算名詞　　参 **It's much fun. = It' a lot of fun.**　すごく楽しい
　※本文では I don't think it's much fun. となっているので、部分否定となり「あまり楽しくないと思う」

☐ **reservation**　レストランや乗り物などの予約
　参 **make a reservation for ~** が慣用。
　※人（お医者さんや弁護士、先生など）に会う予約は appointment を用いる。
　　make an appointment with ~ や make an appointment to see ~ となる。
　　reservation も appointment も可算名詞。

名詞 (2)

TRANSLATION

恵子とジョンは新しいアパートに引っ越したばかりです。
彼らは週末をどのように過ごそうかと思っています。

Keiko: 今週末、街に行って新しいアパートのために家具をいくつか買わない？　今は何もなくてさびしい限りよ。

John: それはいいけど、週末を家具のショッピングに使うのはあまり楽しくないと思うよ。そうだ！　どこかに出かけよう。

Keiko: 本当？　海で2、3日過ごしたいわ。

John: 了解。今すぐビーチフロントホテルに部屋を予約するよ！

WORDS & EXPRESSIONS

- **bare**　形（家やアパートなどに）家具がない、飾りがない
  ※本来は「裸の」という意味。
  例 **His new house looks bare.**　まだ新居には家具がないようだ。
- **shop**　動 – **shop for sth**　買い物をする　～を買う
- **I know!**　そうだ！・よしきた！
- **I'd love to**　～したい　参 **I want to** ～ より丁寧な表現
- **couple**　もとは2つ、現在は **a couple of** で **a few** と同じように「2、3の」の意味で使う
- **I'll ~ right away**　すぐに～するよ

EXPLORING GRAMMAR

advice

英語の名詞には可算名詞（数を数えられる）と不可算名詞（数を数えられない）がある。日本語での判断では使い方を間違えることも多い。

Give me an advice. は間違いで、**Give me some advice.** と冠詞 **an** をとり **some** をつけるか、**Give me a piece of advice.** とする必要がある。

company / office / work

✗ **My father goes to the company at nine.**

☞ company は事業を営む人たちの集合体を意味するので、

My father goes to his office at nine. 父は9時に会社に行く
と office を使うか、

My father goes to work at nine.
とするのが自然。

Which company do you work for?
どちらの会社にお勤めですか

✗ **Which company do you work in?**

salary / wage cost / price

● 日本語ではあまり区別されない語を英会話ではよく間違って使用することがある。

salary　定期的に払われる給料
wage(s)　不定期な（主に）労働に対する賃金
wages　アルバイトなどで受け取る賃金
cost　かかる経費
price　客が払う金額、値段

参 抽象的に **You must pay the price for your mistake.**「そのミスのために後で痛い目に遭うぞ」と脅すこともある。

lightning / thunder

- 「雷」といっても、光る方は lightning、とどろく音の方は thunder。thunder and lightning は「雷鳴」「稲妻」の両方。

a pair of glasses / pants / scissors

- 常に複数で用いる語が英語には多くある。2つひと組のものは a pair of ～で表す

a pair of glasses　眼鏡一つ　　**a pair of pants**　ズボン１本
a pair of scissors　ハサミ１丁
a pair of silk pajamas　シルクのパジャマ１着

など。

economics / physics / politics

economics　経済学　　**physics**　物理学　　**politics**　政治学

のように -s をつける学問もあるが、単数扱いである。

chemistry　化学　　**geography**　地理

のように -s がつかないものもある。

Plural nouns

常に複数形で表記される特殊なものとしては、

belongings　持ち物　　**interests**　利害　　**arms**　武器
means　手段　　**valuables**　貴重品

などがある。

Strategies for the TOEIC

• Choose the correct word or words in brackets ( ).

Can you remember...?

1. My father goes to (work / company / office) at nine.
2. Give me (an advice / a piece of advice / some advices).
3. You must pay the (price / cost / salary) for your mistake.

Can you guess...?

4. I get my (salary / salaries) at the end of the month.
5. Guests can keep their (interests / arms / valuables) in the room safe.
6. At university, my major was (economy / economize / economics).
7. In spring, we usually go to see (cherries / cherry blossoms).
8. I need more (information / informations) about the delay of the plane.
9. My doctor always tells me (fruit is / fruits are) good for my health.
10. I need more (time / times) to finish this exercise.

Answers

1 work **2** a piece of advice **3** price **4** salary
5 valuables **6** economics **7** cherry blossoms **8** information
9 fruit is **10** time

UNIT 14 Participles

- ㉓ **Past participles** … 過去分詞
- ㉔ **Present participles** … 現在分詞

LISTEN & READ

The Browns bought a cheap used car for their travels in Japan. They're preparing to drive to Sendai from Tokyo.

Emily: Dad, you look different.

Trevor: I ㉓**had my hair cut** yesterday, especially for the trip! What do you think?

Georgie: Cool, dad. You look ten years younger.

Angela: Yes, darling. It suits you. By the way, did you ㉓**have the car repaired** yesterday?

Trevor: I sure did. I'll ㉔**get the engine going**. We have a long drive ahead.

Georgie: How long will it take to get to Sendai, Dad?

Trevor: Well, I asked the concierge and he said it takes about six hours, but I'm not sure whether I ㉓**made myself understood**.

Angela: I'm sure you did, honey. The concierge speaks English very well!

NOTES

- **look different** ➡ Unit 9 参照
  - 参 **look ten years younger** 10歳若く見える
  - 同 = look younger by ten years
- **How long will it take to ~** ～するのにどのくらいかかるか
  - 返事 ➡ It takes ~ to get to … …に着くのに～かかる
- **I'm sure you did.** you did は you made yourself understood の言い換え。

100　Unit 14

分詞

TRANSLATION

ブラウン家では日本での旅行のために安い中古車を買いました。彼らは東京から仙台へのドライブの準備をしているところです。

Emily: お父さん、今日は違って見えるわ。

Trevor: 昨日散髪したんだ、旅行のために特別にね！　どう思う？

Georgie: カッコいいよ、お父さん。10歳は若く見えるよ。

Angela: そうよ、あなた。とてもよく似合っているわ。ところで、昨日車を直してもらった？

Trevor: もちろんだよ。エンジンをかけるよ。長い車の旅だからね。

Georgie: お父さん、仙台にはどのくらいで着くの？

Trevor: そうだね、管理人に聞いたんだけど、6時間くらいかかると言っていたが、私の言いたいことが通じたのか自信がないんだ。

Angela: 大丈夫、通じたと思うわ、あなた。管理人は英語がとても上手だから！

WORDS & EXPRESSIONS

- **darling** 名 (夫婦や恋人など) 愛する人への呼びかけ
- **It suits you.** 似合う
- **By the way,** (話題を変えるときに) ところで
- **I sure did.** ちゃんとやりました　参 **surely** を使わないのが"口語"
- **get (sth) going** sth を作動させる
- **ahead** 副 前に・これから
- **concierge** 名 ホテルなどの案内人・管理人 (仏語)
- **make (oneself) understood** 話が通じる・理解してもらえる
- **honey** 名 あなた　※ darling と同じく愛する人への呼びかけ

EXPLORING GRAMMAR

現在分詞（～ing）の用法

You must get the conversation going.
会話をスムーズに進めなくてはいけない

You ought not to leave your baby crying.
赤ちゃんを泣かせたままにしてはいけない

- leave の場合は"～の状態に放っておく"というニュアンス。

Refrain from leaving the engine running in this parking lot.
この駐車場ではエンジンをかけっ放しにするのはお控えください

- keep を用いると"意図的に～の状態にしておく"となる。

Please keep the water running till I say when.
いいと言うまで水は出しっぱなしにしておいてください

I'm very sorry to have kept you waiting so long.
長くお待たせして恐縮です

〈知覚動詞（see, listen to, smell など）＋目的語＋現在分詞〉の用法

I saw my English teacher shopping with his wife.
英語の先生が奥さんと買い物をしているのを見ました

Why don't you listen to the birds singing in the forest?
森の中で鳥が鳴いているのを聞きませんか

When I got home, I smelled something burning in the kitchen.
帰宅したとき、台所で何かが焦げているにおいがした

I felt something crawling on my back.
何かが背中をはっているのを感じた

● それぞれ "目的語が〜しているという状態を知覚する" というのが基本。

Honey, we can't have our daughter idling about all the time.
あなた、娘をいつまでもぶらぶらさせておくわけにはいかないわ

のように用いることもできる。

〈知覚動詞・使役動詞（make など）＋目的語＋過去分詞〉の用法

● 現在分詞と違って、過去分詞の場合は "目的語が動作を受ける" というのが基本。

Did you make yourself understood in English while you were in New York?
ニューヨークにいる間に英語で話が通じましたか

Suddenly I heard my name called in the lobby.
突然ロビーで名前が呼ばれるのが聞こえた

My mother had her hair dyed at the beauty parlor.
母は美容院で髪を染めてもらった

I must have my camera fixed at the manufacturer.
カメラをメーカーで修理してもらわなくてはいけない

など "頼んで〜してもらう" 場合と、

I had my purse stolen in the train.
電車の中で財布を盗まれた

のように "被害" を表す場合がある。

Many of the residents in the area had their roofs blown off by the tornado.
その地域の多くの住民は竜巻に屋根を吹き飛ばされた

〈want ＋目的語＋現在分詞・過去分詞〉の用法

I don't want my daughter staring at strangers like that.
娘には他人をあんな風に見つめてもらいたくない

I want all the e-mails printed before the negotiation.
交渉の前にメールを全部印刷しておいて欲しい

Many movie stars don't want their photos taken on the street without their permission.
多くの映画スターは路上で無断で写真を撮られるのを好まない

STRATEGIES FOR THE TOEIC

CAN YOU REMEMBER...?

• **Choose the correct word or words in brackets ( ).**

1. I saw my English teacher (shop / shopping / shopped) with his wife.
2. You ought not to leave your baby (to cry / crying).
3. I'm very sorry to have kept you (to wait / waiting / waited) so long.
4. I had my purse (stole / stealing / stolen) in the train.
5. Many movie stars don't want their photos (taking / took / taken) on the street without their permission.
6. When I got home, I smelled something (burn / burning) in the kitchen.

CAN YOU GUESS...?

• **Fill the blanks with a form of the verbs in brackets.**

7. Keep _____ and don't turn around or I'll shoot! (walk)
8. Have you ever _____ anything _____ by anybody? (steal)
9. I love listening to the waves _____ against the rocks. (crash)
10. A good teacher can't have his students _____ in class. (sleep)

ANSWERS

1. shopping 2. crying 3. waiting 4. stolen 5. taken
6. burning 7. walking 8. had, stolen 9. crashing 10. sleeping

UNIT 15 *Passive voice*

- ㉕ **Present/Past continuous**…現在／過去進行形の受動態
- ㉖ **Present/Past simple**…現在／過去の受動態

LISTEN & READ

John and Keiko are having breakfast.
They're complaining about the noise.

Keiko: The house next door ㉕**is still being built.** It's so noisy!

John: And what about the noise from last night's party?

Keiko: What party? I didn't hear anything. I slept like a log.

John: You're kidding! I'm sure a party ㉕**was being held** downstairs. I heard lots of music and laughter and clinking of glasses.

Keiko: Well, Japanese houses ㉖**are made of wood and paper,** no wonder you heard everything.

John: Then why didn't *you* hear the noise from the party?

Keiko: Because I wore a pair of earplugs that ㉖**were given to me** by that nice flight attendant when we went to Hawaii last summer!

NOTES

- ☐ **What about~?**　～についてはどうなの？　※意見を求めるときに用いる。
- ☐ **be holding a party**　パーティーを開いている
  - 参 受け身は、**be being held** となる。
- ☐ **downstairs / upstairs**　階下で／階上で
  - ※いずれも副詞（adv）なので前置詞をつけないで使用。

受動態

TRANSLATION

ジョンと恵子は朝食を食べています。彼らは騒音に不平を言っています。

Keiko: 隣のお家はまだ建築中なの。うるさいわね！

John: それと、昨日の夜のパーティーの騒音はどうだった？

Keiko: どこのパーティー？　何も聞こえなかったわ。ぐっすり寝ていたもの。

John: 冗談じゃないよ。下の階で絶対パーティーをやってたよ。音楽や笑い声、グラスのカチャカチャいう音が耳いっぱい聞こえたよ。

Keiko: そうね、日本の家屋は木と紙でできているから、あなたに全部聞こえたのも当たり前ね。

John: じゃあ、どうして君にはパーティーのあの騒音が聞こえなかったの？

Keiko: 去年の夏にハワイに行ったときに親切な客室乗務員がくれた耳栓をしていたおかげよ。

- □ 〈be made of + 材料〉　〜でできている
  - 参 〈be made from + 原料〉　※加工されてもとの姿からは変わっている。
  - 例 **Wine is made from grapes.**　ワインはブドウから作られる
- □ **a pair of 〜**　2つでひと組のもの（既習）
  - 参 **a pair of trousers**　ズボン1本　　**a pair of glasses**　眼鏡一つ
    a pair of scissors　ハサミ1丁　　などに注意。➡ Unit 13 参照

WORDS & EXPRESSIONS

- **I slept like a log.** （丸太のように）ぐっすり眠った
- **You're kidding!** からかっているのか
  ※「冗談だろ！」と驚きを表現する。You must be kidding. とも。
- **laughter** 名笑い声　動 **laugh**
- **clinking of glasses** グラスが触れ合う音
- **no wonder** （〜も驚きではない）どうりで〜
- **flight attendant** 客室乗務員
  ※ stewardess は男性名詞の steward に女性語尾の -ess をつけたものなので、Sexism を考慮して現在は使用が控えられている。

EXPLORING GRAMMAR

受動態〈be ＋過去分詞〉

The house is made of bricks.
その家はレンガ造りだ

The boys broke the window while they were playing baseball.
= **The window was broken by the boys while they were playing baseball.**
少年たちは野球をしているときに、その窓ガラスを割った
☛ 行為者を表記したいときは〈by ＋行為者〉で表す。

進行形の文の受動態〈be ＋ being ＋過去分詞〉

An American corporation is developing the offshore oilfield.
= **The offshore oilfield is being developed by an American corporation.**
その海洋油田はアメリカの企業が開発している

When I entered the conference room, it was still being used by my colleagues.
会議室に入ったら、まだ同僚が使っているところだった

助動詞を含む受動態は助動詞のあと〈be＋過去分詞〉

Students must obey the school regulations.
= The school regulations must be obeyed by students.
校則は守らなくてはいけない

These exam questions cannot be solved in 60 minutes.
この試験問題は60分で解くことはできない

現在完了の受動態は〈have/has＋been＋過去分詞〉

They have recycled the cardboard boxes and PET bottles.
= The cardboard boxes and PET bottles have been recycled.
段ボールやペットボトルはリサイクルされてきている

- idiom が"動作を表す"場合の受動態：
  原則として idiom の形を保ったまま受動態にする。

The family brought up the kitten at home.
= The kitten was brought up by the family at home.
その子猫は自宅で育てられた

It was taken care of mainly by the little girl.
それは主に少女に世話された

It was named after the girl's grandmother.
それはその少女の祖母にちなんで名づけられました

The boys made fun of the kitten.
= The kitten was made fun of by the boys.
男の子たちはその子猫をからかった

注意すべき受動態

● 使役動詞 make を使用する場合

My mother made me do the dishes last night.
昨夜母に皿洗いをさせられた

のように、能動態では to のない不定詞（原形不定詞）を用いる。

受動態になると……
↓
I was made to do the dishes last night by my mother.

と to 不定詞に変わる。

● 疑問詞が行為者を表す場合の受動態

Who sent this letter to you?
= By whom was this letter sent to you?
誰がこの手紙を君に送ったのだ？

のように **By＋whom＋be 動詞＋主語＋過去分詞** の構文になる。最近では、**Who was this letter sent to you by?** として、**by** を後置し、疑問詞に **who** を使うことが増えた。

● 第4文型〈S＋V＋O1＋O2〉の文は受動態に変えるときに O1 も O2 も主語にすることができる。

Mr. Lia teaches us "Communicative English."
= We are taught "Communicative English" by Mr. Lia. /
"Communicative English" is taught us / to us by Mr. Lia.

リア先生は我々に "Communicative English" を教えている

受動態にならない他動詞

- resemble, take after「〜に似ている」は他動詞で目的語をとるが、受動態にはならない。

    My granddaughter resembles her mother.
    孫娘は母親に似ている

    ✗ Her mother is resembled by my granddaughter.

    他にも、下記のような他動詞は受動態にならないので注意が必要。

- have：所有している

    He has a huge mansion.　彼の邸宅は巨大だ

- fit：似合う

    This dress sure fits you.　そのドレス本当に似合っているよ

- lack：欠けている

    Too bad he lacks common sense.
    彼には常識がないのが残念だ

- stand：我慢する

    I can no longer stand this noise.
    この騒音にはこれ以上我慢できない

その他 **enter**「〜に入る」、**escape**「〜を免れる」なども受動態にならないので注意が必要。

Strategies for the TOEIC

Can you remember...?

• **Fill the blanks with a passive form of the verbs in brackets.**

1. The house _____ of bricks. (make)
2. The offshore oilfield is _____ by an American corporation. (develop)
3. When I entered the conference room, it _____ still _____ by my colleagues. (use)
4. The kitten was _____ by the family at home. (bring up)
5. I _____ to do the dishes last night by my mother. (make)
6. We _____ "Communicative English" by Mr. Lia. (teach)

Can you guess...?

• **Fill the blanks with a passive form.**

7. I _____ in Italy, but I grew up in England. (be born)
8. I had my wallet _____ while I was on holiday last year! (steal)
9. This ring _____ of solid gold. (make)
10. My name's Joseph. I _____ after my grandfather. (name)

Answers

1 is made   **2** being developed   **3** was, being used
4 brought up   **5** was made   **6** are taught   **7** was born
8 stolen   **9** is made   **10** was named

UNIT 16 Phrasal verbs

㉗ Idiomatic phrasal verbs…慣用句動詞

LISTEN & READ

Maki and Kate are talking about Maki's grandma.

Maki: I'm really **looking forward** to seeing my grandma in the holidays. I've been **putting it off** for too long.

Kate: She **took care of** you when you were little while your parents were working, right?

Maki: Yes. I really **look up to** her. But, to be honest, she was always very strict with me. She would always **find fault with** everything I did.

Kate: Well, it **paid off**. Look at you now!

Maki: Yes, I guess I've **turned out alright**!

NOTES

- **to be honest** 正直に言うと 不定詞の独立用法
  - 参 **to be frank with you** 率直に言って
  - **to do him justice** 彼を正当に判断すると 慣用表現

- **She would always ~** いつも~したものだ
  ※この would は「過去の反復動作」を表す。
  - 参 **used to ~** 長期にわたる動作・過去の状態

句動詞

TRANSLATION

麻紀とケイトは麻紀のおばあさんのことを話しています。

- Maki: 休暇におばあちゃんに会いに行くのを本当に楽しみにしているわ。先延ばしにしすぎていたの。
- Kate: ご両親が共働きだったあなたが小さいときに面倒をみてくれたのよね？
- Maki: そうよ。尊敬しているわ。でも、正直に言うといつも厳しかったのよ。私のすることになんでもあらさがしをしたのよ。
- Kate: それがうまくいったのよね。今のあなたを見てみなさいよ！
- Maki: そうね、うまくいったのね！

WORDS & EXPRESSIONS

- **look forward to ~ing** 〜するのを楽しみにしている
- **put off** 延期する 同＝ **postpone**
  ※いずれも動詞が目的語の場合は put off ~ing のように動名詞になる。
- **take care of** 〜の世話をする 同＝ **look after**
- **look up to** 〜を尊敬する 同＝ **respect**
- **find fault with** 〜のあらさがしをする 類≒ **criticize** 批判する
- **pay off** （努力などが）効果をもたらす、報われる
- **turn out** 〜であることがわかる

EXPLORING GRAMMAR

句動詞の注意事項

I have to put off our departure for the peak until the clouds drift away.
雲が切れるまで頂上への出発を延期しなくてはいけない

- departure が代名詞 it に変わる場合は、off（副詞）を代名詞の後に置かなくてはいけない。

I have to put it off until next morning.

参 **take off** 脱ぐ　なども同じ。

Why don't we take off our shoes before entering this place?
ここに入る前に靴を脱いだらどうだろう

代名詞なら……
↓
Why don't we take them off before entering this place?

となる。

前置詞によって意味が変わる句動詞にも注意

① ask for ～：～を求める　ask after ～：～の体調・安否を尋ねる

How dare you ask for such a large amount of money?
よくもそんな大金をくれと言えるね

My wife asked after her father's health by phone.
妻は父親の体調（容態）を電話で尋ねた

② deal with ～：～を扱う　deal in ～：（商品を）扱う

They deal in used cars at that shop.
あの店では中古車を扱っている

Deal with this package with care.
この小包は取り扱い注意です

③ succeed in ～：～で成功する　succeed to ～：～を継承する

My son will succeed to my position in this company.
息子がこの会社の跡を継いでくれる

④ agree to ～：（事柄に）同意する　agree with ～：（人に）同意する
agree on ～：合意点が見つかる

How did those companies agree on the merger?
あれらの会社がよく合併に同意しましたね

⑤ call at ～：（場所を）を訪ねる　call on ～：（人を）訪問する
call for ～：～を要求する

会話に頻出の句動詞（群動詞）

● 〈動詞＋前置詞〉の形

① come across ～：～に偶然会う・～を（偶然）見つける

Where did you come across this rare camera?
こんな珍しいカメラをどこで見つけたのですか

② come down with ～：（病気など）にかかる

I came down with this cold when I walked in the rain.
雨の中を歩いていてこの風邪をひきました

③ go on ～ing：～し続ける　＝ continue ～ing

He went on talking about his journey until midnight.
彼は深夜まで旅について話し続けた

④ go at ~ : ~に取りかかる、~に襲いかかる

Finally they went at their work in earnest.
ついに彼らは真剣に仕事に取り組み始めた

⑤ get to ~ : ~に取りかかる・~に到着する

Could you tell me how to get to your place from the station?
駅から君のところへの行き方を教えてくれますか

⑥ get at ~ : ~を理解する、~に連絡する

Why not get at him when you can?
できるときに彼に連絡しては?

⑦ belong to ~ : ~に所属する

What club did you belong to at school?
学校では何部でしたか

⑧ look for ~ : ~を探す

What are you looking for here?
ここで何を探しているのですか

⑨ look into ~ : ~を調査する

The committee gave us a pledge to look into the cause of the accident.
委員会は事故の原因を調査することを約束した

⑩ look after ~ : ~を世話する　= take care of ~

Who will look after your parents when they get sick?
親御さんが病気になったら誰が面倒を見るんですか

⑪ account for 〜：〜を説明する　＝ explain

⑫ add to 〜：〜を増やす

⑬ care for 〜：〜を気に入る　＝ like

⑭ depend on 〜：〜に頼る・〜次第だ

⑮ take after 〜：〜に似ている　＝ resemble

● 〈動詞＋副詞〉の形（自動詞の場合：目的語をとらない）

My computer broke down all of a sudden.
コンピュータが突然壊れた

In spite of the citizens' objections, the war broke out.
市民の反対にもかかわらず、戦争がついに始まった

How did that incident come about?
その事件はどのようにして起こったのか

I just dropped by to say hello.　挨拶に立ち寄っただけだよ

Where should I get off to visit the National Museum?
国立博物館に行くにはどこで降りればいいですか

Don't stay up till late at night!　夜遅くまで起きていてはいけません

Forget it. It turned out all right.
もういいよ。大丈夫だとわかったんだから

Hurry up, or you'll miss the train.
急いで、さもないと列車に遅れるよ

Finally the actress showed up.　とうとうその女優が姿を現した

● 〈動詞＋副詞〉の形（他動詞の場合：目的語をとる）

I would like my employees to carry out their mission.
従業員には任務を遂行してもらいたい

I was born and brought up in Yokkaichi.
生まれも育ちも四日市です

Sometimes she puts on airs and that's why some of us don't take to her.
時々彼女は気取るんです、だから気に入らない人もいます

Since it is raining so hard we have to call off our picnic today. = cancel
大雨だから今日のピクニックは中止しなくてはいけない

You are supposed to hand (turn) in your report by the deadline.
締め切りまでにレポートを提出することになっています

hand in~, turn in~   = submit~   ～を提出する

You must not make up an excuse for coming late.
遅刻の弁解をでっちあげてはいけません

I couldn't make out / understand what he was talking about because he spoke very fast.
彼は早口だったので、何を言っているのか理解することができなかった

It's merciless of you to turn down her request flatly.
彼女の要望をきっぱりと断ったのは無情ですよ

I know you are wealthy, but you should not show it off.
君が裕福なのは分っているが、それを見せびらかすべきではない

● 〈動詞＋副詞＋前置詞〉の形

How can you put up with your son's rudeness?
君の息子の無礼さをよく**我慢する**ことができるね

We are going to put up at a small inn in Hakone.
箱根の小さな旅館に**泊まる**つもりだ

Too bad I can't go out with you. I have to catch up on my assignment.
残念だが君と**出かける**ことができない。課題の遅れを**取り戻さ**なくてはいけないんだ

I must stop by a gas station, because we are running out of gas.
ガスが**なくなる**からガソリンスタンドに寄らなくては

We should not look down on a person because he is poor.
貧しいという理由で人を**さげすんで**はいけない
反 look up to ~ ＝ respect~ 　~を尊敬する

How will that company make up for the loss?
あの会社はどうやって損失を**埋め合わせる**だろうか

They should do away with this old-fashioned system.
この流行遅れのシステムを**廃止する**べきだ

● 〈動詞＋名詞＋前置詞〉の形

Are you going to take part in that business?
君はあの仕事に**参加する**つもりですか

The pilot lost control of the plane.
パイロットは飛行機の**制御**ができなくなった

The policemen lost sight of the criminal in the dark.
警官たちは暗闇の中で犯人を見失った
反 catch sight of~　～(の姿)を見つける

● 〈動詞＋再帰代名詞(-self, -selves)＋前置詞〉の形

Meals and drinks are over there. Help yourself to whatever you like.
食事と飲み物はあちらにあります。お好きなものを召し上がれ

The CEO abandoned himself to despair.
社長は自暴自棄になった

Most of them adapted themselves to a new environment.
彼らの大部分は新しい環境に順応した

Students should devote themselves to their studies.
学生は学問に専念するべきだ

STRATEGIES FOR THE TOEIC

CAN YOU REMEMBER...?

- **Choose the correct word or words in brackets ( ).**

1 Why don't we (put / take / leave) off our shoes before entering this place?

2 My wife asked (after / before / during) her father's health by phone.

3 I was born and (raised / grown / brought) up in Yokkaichi.

4. Sometimes she puts (up / on / off) airs and that's why some of us don't take (at / to / for) her.
5. We should not look down (to / in / on) a person because he is poor.
6. Students should devote (themselves / theirselves) to their studies.

CAN YOU GUESS…?

- **Fill the blanks with a phrasal verb from the box that has the same meaning as the words in brackets.**

drop in on / keep up / came up with / look up

7. She was the one who (thought of) _____ the idea!
8. If you're in the neighborhood, please (come and visit) _____ us.
9. I'll (search for the meaning of) _____ the word in my dictionary.
10. Your grades are improving. (Continue) _____ the good work!

ANSWERS

1. take   2. after   3. brought   4. on, to   5. on   6. themselves
7. came up with   8. drop in on   9. look up   10. Keep up

UNIT 17 Prepositions

㉘ Prepositions…前置詞

LISTEN & READ

Trevor meets Tim, a tourist from America, in a pub in Shinjuku. They are drinking beer.

Tim: So, Trevor. What do you do?

Trevor: I work ㉘**for a small computer company** ㉘**in London**, established almost twenty years ago ㉘**by my father**. How about you, Tim?

Tim: I work ㉘**at a university** ㉘**in California**. I lecture ㉘**in American cinema**.

Trevor: Really? I'm taking my wife to see a movie tonight! There's a romantic comedy ㉘**on at the theater** ㉘**next to our hotel**.

Tim: What's it called?

Trevor: It's called *I've never been* ㉘*to Paris*. Oh, is that the time? I'd better get back ㉘**to the hotel** or we won't be ㉘**in time** for the start of the movie. Nice meeting you, Tim.

Tim: Likewise. Enjoy the movie!

NOTES

☐ **work for~** 〜で働いている
　※「会社」が後にくる場合は"場所を表す"atやinではなくforを用いることで「役に立っている」「貢献している」というニュアンスを表す。work at a university はその大学で「何をしているか」は明示されず、後のI lecture〜で「教えている」ことを説明している。

☐ **I'm taking my wife** ※進行形でtonightを伴うことで"予定"を表す。

☐ **be on at ~**　〜で上演している　※onだけでplayingの意味を持つ。

☐ **What is it called?**　それは何と呼ばれているの？・題名は？
　同 = **What's the title of the movie?**

前置詞

TRANSLATION

トレバーはアメリカからの旅行者のティムに新宿のパブで会っています。彼らはビールを飲んでいます。

Tim: ところで、トレバー、仕事は何をしていますか。

Trevor: 父が20年ほど前に始めたロンドンの小さなコンピュータ会社で働いているんだよ。君はどうだい、ティム？

Tim: カリフォルニアの大学で働いているよ。アメリカの映画について講義しているんだ。

Trevor: 本当かい？　今夜妻を映画に連れていくんだよ。ホテルの隣の劇場でロマンチックコメディをやっているんだ。

Tim: 題名は何？

Trevor: 『パリには行ったことがない』だよ。おや、もう時間だね。ホテルに戻らないと、映画の開始に間に合わないよ。会えて良かったよ、ティム。

Tim: こちらこそ。映画を楽しんでね！

WORDS & EXPRESSIONS

- **established** 動 設立された　※過去分詞で前の company を修飾している
- **How about you?** 君はどうですか
- **lecture** 動 講義する
- **American cinema** アメリカ映画
  ※cinema、film は主にイギリス英語で、米語では movie を使うことが多い。
- **Is that the time?** もうこんな時間？ 慣用表現
- **I'd better ~** そろそろ～しなくては
- **Nice meeting you.** 会えて良かった　※話が終わって別れるときに用いる。
  参 (It's) Nice to meet you. は "ここから話が始まるとき" に使う。
- **Likewise.** 同じようにあなたにもね　参 Same here! とも言う。

Exploring grammar

前置詞の基本的用法（場所を表す主な前置詞）

I'll meet you at the station.
駅で出迎えます
- ☛ at は比較的小さい「点」のような場所を指す。

Not a footstep was to be seen on the ground.
地面には足跡は見当たらなかった
- ☛ on には「接触」の意味がある。地面に「接触」するというニュアンス。

Hang that picture on the wall.
その絵を壁にかけなさい

I found a fly on the ceiling.
ハエが天井にいるのを見つけた
- 参 on the desk などから推量される「天井の上」は正しくない。

How about throwing a potluck party at my place?
家で持ち寄りパーティーを開くのはどうですか

We have lived in Tokyo for 2 decades.
東京に20年間住んでいます
- ☛ in は「広がりを持った場所の中」という意味。

● 他に注意を要する

over、under、above、below、beneath などの前置詞がある。

A helicopter is hovering over the volcano.
ヘリコプターが火山上空をホバリングしている
- ☛ over は「～の（真）上に」「～を覆って」の意。

The cat is sleeping under the table.
その猫はテーブルの下で寝ている
- ☛ under は「～の（真）下に」を表す。

Machu Picchu, the ancient city in Peru, is 2,430 meters above sea level.
ペルーの古代都市、マチュピチュは海抜2,430メートルのところにある
☛ above は「〜より（位置が）上」という意味で必ずしも「真上」を表しているわけではなく、また on のように「接触」はしていない。

He is above telling a lie. 　彼は嘘をつくような人ではない
☛ 抽象的に用いることもできる。
反 **above ≒ below** 　〜より（位置が）下

My son is below average in height.
息子は身長が平均より下だ

● near、by、beside は「位置が近い」ことを表す。near は漠然と「近い」ことを表し、by は「すぐそばに」、beside は「そばに並んで」という違いを表す。

The residential area is located near the station.
その住宅地は駅の近くにある

I put the flower pot by the window.
窓辺に植木鉢を置いた

My girlfriend sat beside me in my car.
ガールフレンドは車の中で私の隣に座った

前置詞の基本的用法（勘違いしやすい前置詞）

● besides「〜の他に、〜に加えて」を表す。
idiom で言えば in addition to 〜と表す意味は同じ。

Besides (= In addition to) math, Hanako is good at history.
華子は数学の他に、歴史が得意です

- between と among は（人）数の違いで使い分ける。２人（つ）の場合は between、３人（つ）以上の場合は among を用いる。

   This is between you and me, but I'm engaged.
   ここだけの話だけど、私婚約したの
   同 ＝ This is between us

   That singer is popular among young girls.
   あの歌手は若い女性の間で人気がある

- 「～のあたりを」「～のあちこちを」は around [round] で表すが、ほぼ似たような意味を about で表すことがある（主にイギリス英語）。

   I've got a pain around the abdomen.
   腹部のあたりが痛い

   Don't beat around the bush! 比喩的
   遠回しな言い方をしないで

   The dog was walking about the room.
   その犬は部屋を歩き回っていた

前置詞の基本的用法（時を表す主な前置詞）

My daughter was born on 12th of February in 1992.
娘は1992年の2月12日生まれだ
　☛ "日" には on、年号には in を用いる。

Give me a call at 3 o'clock.
３時に電話をちょうだい
　☛ 時間には at を使う。

- 慣用的に

    in the morning / evening　午前中に／夕方に
    at noon / night　正午に／夜に
    ☛ 他には at Christmas　クリスマスに　　at Easter　イースターに

    Long skirts were in fashion in 1970's.
    ロングスカートは1970年代に流行った

    I'm going out, but I'll be back in a few hours.
    出かけるけれど、2、3時間で戻ります
    ☛ in は「(未来の)時間の経過」を表し、「過去」の場合は after を用いる。

    He went out, and came back after three hours.
    彼は出かけて3時間後に戻った

- by と till / until は区別が必要。by は「〜までに」と完了の期限を表し、till / until は「〜までの継続」を表す。

    You are to submit your essay by next Monday.
    次の月曜日までにエッセイを出すことになっていますよ

    We had lived in Hamamatsu till our father got a job in Tokyo.
    父が東京で仕事を得るまでは浜松に住んでいた

- for は「(不特定な期間)の間」、during は「(特定の期間)の間じゅう、〜の間のどこかで」を表す。

    I'm sorry to have kept you waiting for such a long time.
    こんなに長く待たせてごめんなさい

    We visited Niigata during my winter vacation.
    冬休みの間に新潟を訪れた

前置詞の基本的用法（その他重要な前置詞）

Today's dinner is on me.
今日の夕食は私のおごりです

The beauty of the scenery was beyond description.
景色の美しさは表現できないほどだった

After you, please. お先にどうぞ

What's on at that theater? あの劇場では何を上演していますか

What are you here for? ここにどのような用事ですか

To my surprise, he was arrested for murder.
驚いたことに彼は殺人で逮捕された

For here or to go?
こちらでお召し上がりですか、それともお持ち帰りですか

To avoid inhaling the exhaust gas, she went out with a mask on.
排気ガスを吸うのを避けるために彼女はマスクを着けて外出した

They are paid by the week. 彼らは週給だ

The ship wrecked off the coast of Sanriku.
その船は三陸沖で難破した

The time of arrival depends on the traffic.
到着時間は交通（状況）次第です

He was fined for speeding. 彼はスピード違反で罰金を科せられた

Our plane took off thirty minutes behind schedule.
私たちの（乗った）飛行機は予定より30分遅れで離陸した

Strategies for the TOEIC

Can you remember...?

• **Choose the correct word or words in brackets ( ).**

1. Machu Picchu, the ancient city in Peru, is 2,430 meters (over / above) sea level.
2. That singer is popular (in / between / among) young girls.
3. My daughter was born (in / on / at) 12th of February (in / on / at) 1992.
4. I'm going out, but I'll be back (in / after / over) a few hours.
5. You are to submit your essay (by / until / on) next Monday.
6. To avoid inhaling the exhaust gas, she went out (in / for / with) a mask on.

Can you guess...?

• **Fill the blanks with a preposition from the box.**

under / by / until / on / with / during / in / at / for

7. I was born _____ a Saturday _____ August _____ 1964.
8. We need to finish this project _____ the end of October, so we have to work _____ the holidays.
9. You shouldn't dine _____ an elegant restaurant _____ a hat on!
10. The noise woke me up _____ 4 o'clock _____ the morning.

Answers

1. above 2. among 3. on, in 4. in 5. by 6. with
7. on, in, in 8. by, during 9. in / at, with 10. at, in

UNIT 18 Pronouns

- ㉙ **Indefinite pronouns**…不定代名詞
- ㉚ **Possessive pronouns and adjectives**…所有代名詞／形容詞

LISTEN & READ

Keiko is looking forward to her class reunion.

Keiko: ㉙**All** of ㉚**my** friends in ㉚**our** final class at high school are going to the class reunion tonight! I can't wait to see them!

John: Really? ㉙**None** of my friends attended ㉚**mine** last year. It was really boring!

Keiko: I guess ㉙**some** class reunions are fun, while ㉙**others** are terrible. Also, ㉚**my** friends are reliable, while ㉚**yours** are unreliable.

John: Actually, ㉙**most** of ㉚**my** friends are OK, though I must admit, ㉙**some** are pretty selfish. Anyway, have a nice time. I guess I'll get a Chinese.

NOTES

☐ **None of my friends attended mine last year.**
　※ none は「一人も〜ない」という代名詞、mine は my class reunion「僕の方の同窓会」を表す所有代名詞。

☐ **Some are fun while others are terrible.**
　※ while は「〜の一方で」と対比を表すときに用いる。

☐ **Have a nice time!** 楽しんできてね
　※出かける人に用いる表現「行ってらっしゃい」の意。

代名詞

TRANSLATION

恵子は同窓会を楽しみにしています。

Keiko: 高校の最後のクラスの友達みんなが今夜同窓会に行くのよ。待ちきれないわ。

John: 本当？ 僕の同窓会では去年は友達は一人も参加しなかったよ。本当につまらなかった。

Keiko: 同窓会は楽しいのもあるけどひどいのもあるわね。それに、私の友達はあなたの友達と違って信頼できるのよ。

John: 実は、たいていの友達はいいんだけど、わがままなやつもいることは認めなくてはね。とにかく、楽しんできてね。僕は中華料理でもとろうかな。

WORDS & EXPRESSIONS

- **class reunion** 同窓会
- **reliable** 形 信頼できる
- **unreliable** 形 信頼できない 反 reliable
- **I must admit,…** …と認めなくてはいけない・たしかに…だけどね
- **pretty** 副 かなり〜　と形容詞、副詞を強める。
- **selfish** 形 わがままな
- **a Chinese** 中華料理 同 = a Chinese meal / dish

EXPLORING GRAMMAR

注意すべき代名詞の用法

- **Some vs. Others**　母集団が複数名詞で、その中に「〜のものもあれば」また「他には〜のものもある」という対比する表現

We have 50 students in my class; some are diligent, while others are lazy.
クラスには50人の学生がいる。勤勉な学生もいるが、怠惰なものもいる
　☞ この場合 diligent でも lazy でもない学生が50人の中にいることになる。

Some are diligent, while others are lazy, and the others are lukewarm.
勤勉な学生もいるが、怠惰な学生もいる、他の（すべての）学生はどっちつかず（中途半端）だ
　☞ 50人全員について述べている。

対比の表現として用いる場合は……
↓
Some are diligent, some are lazy.
勤勉なものもいるが怠惰なものもいる
　☞ 両方に some を用いることもある。

- **One vs. The other vs. Another**　2つのもの（人）の間の対比の表現

I have two uncles; one is a physician and the other is a dentist.
伯父が二人いるが、一人は内科医でもう一人は歯科医だ
　☞ other(s) に the がつくと残りの全てを表すのは上記と同じ。

3人以上いる場合は……
↓
We have three foreign groups to visit our university; one is from Taiwan, another is from Singapore and the other is from Thailand.

うちの大学には海外から３グループの訪問がある；一つは台湾から、もう一つはシンガポール、あと一つはタイからです
  ☛ another を用いるとその後にまだ"候補"があることを示す。最後の一つはやはり the other となる。

- None「一人も～ない」「一つも～ない」

後に「～を除いて」の **but** を伴い「…以外の誰も～ない」と強調した文に用いることがある。

None but the brave deserves the fair.
勇者だけが美女を得ることができる〈John Dryden (1631-1700)〉

- 可算名詞に用いる none の場合は動詞も口語では複数（この場合 were）を用いる。formal な文では単数扱いにする。不可算名詞に none を用いる場合は単数扱い。

None of the climbers were injured in the avalanche.
登山者の誰も雪崩で負傷しなかった

None of the information was of use.
情報は全く役に立たなかった

- "人"に関しては No one も同じ意味で使える。

No one knows what will happen in the future.
将来何が起こるかは誰にも分らない

- None of your lip! : へらず口をたたくな
  None of your cheek! : 生意気言うな　などのような慣用表現もある。

All vs. Each

- all は"全体をひとまとめ"にして「すべて・みな」を指す。後にくるものによって動詞は単数・複数に合わせる。

  All the money of the aged couple was stolen.
  老夫婦のお金全部が盗まれた

  All the students were satisfied with the results of the research.
  学生全員が調査結果に満足した

- each は"多くの人や物のうち"「一つ一つ全てが」の意味を表す。従って動詞は単数扱いになる。

  Each of the three is different from the other two.
  三者三様である　※ the other については上述。

  To each his own.　人はそれぞれ　（諺）蓼食う虫も好き好き

- all、each が「全て」を表す一方、most は「たいていの〜」を表す。

  Most of the girl students want to wear skirts for the ceremony.
  たいていの女子学生は式典に際してスカートをはくことを望んでいる

  後にくるものが不可算名詞の場合は……
  ↓
  Most of the information he gave us was false.
  彼がよこした情報のほとんどが偽りだった

  のように単数で扱う。

その他 代名詞の慣用表現

I got the news the other day.　先日その知らせを受けました

Allen and Susan love each other.
アレンとスーザンはお互いに愛し合っている

We have to help one another.
お互いに（3人以上）助け合わなくてはね

I go to see movies every other day.
1日おきに映画を見に行きます

On (the) one hand, I would like to assist you, but on the other hand I want you to live on your own.
一方で支援してあげたいが、他方で自立してもらいたいとも思う

Don't ask me one question after another.
次から次に質問しないでくれ

Refrain from speaking ill of others. 他人の悪口は控えなさい

所有代名詞／独立所有格の用法

● mine、yours、his、hers、theirs などがそれぞれあとにくる名詞を略して"独立して"用いることができる。

Tom says he likes my new car, but I love his.
彼は僕の新車が好きと言ってくれるが、僕は彼の車が大好きだ
参 his ＝ his car

I'll tell you my e-mail address, so tell me yours.
僕のメールアドレスを言うから、君のを教えてね

Even if you don't have your own house, you should not envy theirs.
マイホームがないとしても彼らのもの（家）をうらやむべきではない
参 theirs ＝ their house(s)

STRATEGIES FOR THE TOEIC

CAN YOU REMEMBER…?

• Fill the blanks with words from this unit.

1 We have 50 students in my class; _____ are diligent, while others are lazy and _____ are lukewarm.

2 I got the news _____ day.

3 On the one hand, I would like to assist you, but _____ hand I want you to live on your own.

4 _____ of your cheek!

5 Each of the three is different from _____ two.

6 I'll tell you my e-mail address, so tell me _____.

7 **Can you remember the possessive pronouns of these possessive adjectives?**

my = _____ / your = _____ / their = _____ / her = _____

CAN YOU GUESS…?

• Fill the blanks with a form of 'other'.

8 I met an old friend _____ day.

9 That cupcake was delicious. Can I have _____ one?

10 Tom is often kind, _____ hand, he's sometimes selfish.

Answers

1. some, the others
2. the other
3. on the other
4. None
5. the other
6. yours
7. mine, yours, theirs, hers
8. the other
9. another
10. on the other

UNIT 19 Questions

- ㉛ Direct questions … 直接疑問文
- ㉜ "How" questions … How を使った疑問文
- ㉝ Indirect / Negative / Tag questions … 間接疑問文／否定疑問文／付加疑問文

LISTEN & READ

Maki has brought some books from her parents' house. She has parked the car outside her apartment. She asks Kate for help to carry a heavy bag.

Maki: Kate! ㉛**Can you do me a favor?**
㉛**Can you help me carry this bag to my room?**

Kate: Sure, I can. Huh? ㉜**How much** does it weigh? 100 kilograms? ㉝**I wanna know** what you've got in it!

Maki: Just books.

Kate: Books? ㉝**Don't you** already have a million books in your room? ㉝**You don't** need more, **do you?** Phew! Made it!

Maki: Thanks, Kate. Now, let's get another bag from the car.

Kate: Another bag? ㉜**How many** bags have you got?

NOTES

- **Can you do me a favor?**　お願いがあるのですが？
- **do ~ a favor**　～のお願いを聞いてあげる
- **help~ …**　～が…するのを手助けする
- **Huh?**　エッ、ハァ・何だって？　驚きを表す
- **Funny, huh?**　おかしいでしょ
  ※"付加疑問"の代わりに「～でしょう？　～だよね？」として用いられる
- **How much does it weigh?**　どのくらいの重さがあるか？
  ※ weigh は自動詞で「～の重さがある」。失礼を承知で聞くならば、How much do you weigh?「体重はどれくらいですか」とか、This machine weighs more than 10 kilograms.「この機械は10キロ以上の重さです」のように用いる。

疑問文

TRANSLATION

麻紀は実家から本を運んできました。
彼女は車を自分のアパートの外に駐車しました。
彼女はケイトに重いバッグを運ぶ手伝いを頼みます。

Maki: ケイト！　お願い！　このバッグを部屋まで運ぶのを手伝ってくれない？

Kate: もちろんいいわよ。エー！　どれだけ重いの？　100キロ？　何が入っているのか知りたいわ！

Maki: ただ、本よ。

Kate: 本ですって？　もう部屋には100万冊は持っているわよね？　これ以上要らないでしょ？　やれやれ！　運んだわよ！

Maki: ありがとう、ケイト。さて、もう一つバッグを車から運びましょう。

Kate: もう一つですって？　いったいいくつバッグがあるのよ？

WORDS & EXPRESSIONS

- **wanna**　want to~ の口語用法
- **Phew!**　息を吹きながらヒューと音を出すことで、「安心・疲れ・驚き・嫌悪」を表す。
- **Made it!** = (I) Made it.　「やり遂げた」のニュアンス。
  - 例 **Can you make it?**　参加できる？・間に合う？・うまくやれそう？という便利な表現。

Exploring grammar

疑問文の基本

● be 動詞を用いる場合

Tom is tall. → Is Tom tall? の語順にする。
返事は Yes, he is. / No, he isn't.

You are from Japan.　日本から来ています
➡ Are you from Japan?
　Yes, I am. / No, I'm not.

● 一般動詞の場合

She has a large amount of money.　多くのお金を持っています
➡ Does she have a large amount of money?
　Yes, she does. / No, she doesn't.

They live in Tokyo.　東京に住んでいます
➡ Do they live in Tokyo?
　Yes, they do. / No, they don't.

● 助動詞の場合

He can speak French.　フランス語が話せます
➡ Can he speak French?
　Yes, he can. / No, he can't / cannot.

You can play the guitar.　ギターが弾けます
➡ Can you play the guitar?
　Yes, I can. / No, I can't / cannot.

● 少し注意が必要な助動詞の文

Must I go right now? No, you don't have to / you need not.
今すぐ行かなくてはいけませんか？／いいえ、その必要はありません
　➡ Yes, you must.　はい、必要です

Can you ~? には「~できますか」のほかに"許可"を求めることもできる。

Can I keep this pen? このペンもらってもいいですか

Can you give me a hand? ちょっと手を貸してくれませんか

否定疑問の場合；

Aren't you hungry? おなかすいていませんか
➡ **Yes, I am.** すいている／**No, I'm not.** すいていない

日本語で考えると Yes と No を間違えることがある。

Don't you like raw fish? 生魚（刺し身）は嫌いですか
➡ **Yes, I do.** 好き／**No, I don't.** 嫌い

● "疑問"と"確認"を表す付加疑問文

You like seafood salad, don't you?
シーフードサラダは好きでしょう？
➡ **Yes, I do.／No, I don't.**

You can swim a long distance, can't you?
長距離を泳げますよね？
➡ **Yes, I can.／No, I can't / cannot.**

"疑問"の場合は文の最後を上げ調子（rising intonation）で、"確認"の場合は下げ調子（falling intonation）で言うことに注意。

He cannot help us, can he? 彼は私たちを助けられないですよね？
➡ **Yes, he can.** できる／**No, he can't / cannot.** できない

Let's go for a spin. など Let's で始まる文には、shall we? と同意を求める付加疑問にする。

Let's go for a spin, shall we? ドライブに行きましょうよね
➡ **Yes, let's.／No, let's not.**

命令文のときは、依頼を表す will you? をつけ加える。

Carry this bag to my room, will you?
このバッグを部屋まで運んでくれるよね？

● How を用いる疑問文

How are you doing?
元気ですか

I'm good / fine. 元気よ　　**How about you?**　あなたは？
➡ 最近では "How are you?" "I'm fine. Thank you. And you?" よりよく使われる。

"数" を尋ねるときは、

How many books a month do you read?
月に何冊本を読みますか

I read at least three books.　少なくとも３冊読みます

"頻度" を聞くときは、

How often do you practice kendo?
剣道はどのくらい練習しますか

Usually twice a week.　たいてい週に２回です

"量" などは

How much does this fridge weigh?
この冷蔵庫はどのくらいの重さですか

It weighs around 40 kilograms.　40キロくらいでしょう

How much do I owe you?
いくらですか（値段や借りているお金を尋ねる）

"距離"は

How far is it to the theater from here?
ここから劇場まではどのくらいですか

It's about 200 meters. 200メートルくらいです

It's less than twenty minutes' walk.
歩いて20分かかりませんよ

"時間"は How long で尋ねる。

How long does it take to go to Hokkaido by plane?
北海道まで飛行機だとどのくらいかかりますか

I think it takes about three hours.
3時間くらいだと思いますよ

How tall are you? は「身長」を尋ねるのに対して、How tall you are! は「君はなんて背が高いんだ」と感嘆文であることに注意。

How deep ～？ は「深さ」を How high ～？ は「高さ」

How fast is your car? 君の車はどのくらいスピードが出るの

間接疑問文は疑問文を伝える

●疑問詞がある場合はその疑問詞を接続のために使う。

I don't know + What will the weather be like tomorrow?
= I don't know what the weather will be like tomorrow.
明日天気がどのようになるかはわからない

☛ 間接疑問文は平叙文の語順になることに注意。

Tell me + What time is it now?
= Tell me what time it is now.
今何時か教えてください

**I wonder + How long will it take to get to the theater?
= I wonder how long it will take to get to the theater.**
劇場に着くのにどのくらいかかるかしら

● 疑問詞がない場合は if や whether で文をつなげる。

**Do you know? + Will the princess show up at the banquet?
= Do you know if / whether the princess will show up at the banquet?**
王女様が宴に出られるかどうか分かりますか

I want to know + Has the maid cleaned our room yet? = I want to know if / whether the maid has cleaned our room yet.
メイドが部屋を掃除し終えたかどうかを知りたい

伝える部分が過去形になった場合は "時制の一致" が必要。

They wanted to ask + You bought the ticket at the designated ticket window. = They wanted to ask if you had bought the ticket at the designated ticket window.
彼らは君が指定された窓口でチケットを買ったかどうかを尋ねたかった

STRATEGIES FOR THE TOEIC

• Fill the blanks with words from this unit.

CAN YOU REMEMBER...?

1. "You like seafood salad, _____ you?" "Yes, I do."
2. They wanted to ask _____ you had bought the ticket at the designated ticket window.
3. _____ is it to the theater from here?
4. I wonder _____ it will take to get to the theater.
5. I want to know _____ the maid has cleaned our room yet.
6. Let's go for a spin, _____ we?

CAN YOU GUESS...?

7. Negative question: "_____ you Japanese?" "Yes, I am."
8. Direct question: "_____ you swim?" "Well, I could when I was younger."
9. Tag question: "Your dad _____ like French food, _____ he?" "No. In fact, he hates it!"
10. 'How' question: "_____ do you listen to music?" "Every day!"

ANSWERS

1. don't 2. if / whether 3. How far 4. how long 5. if / whether
6. shall 7. Aren't 8. Can 9. doesn't, does / does, doesn't
10. How often

147

UNIT 20 Relative pronouns

㉞ Relative pronouns…関係代名詞

LISTEN & READ

The Browns are having breakfast at their hotel.

Emily: Georgie, you shouldn't eat so many croquettes!

Georgie: But they're so good!

Angela: Emily's right, dear. My mom always used to say, "㉞**You are what you eat**".

Trevor: Well, you're in great shape, Angela. ㉞**What your mom said turns out to be true.**

Angela: Yes, I've always tried hard to follow a healthy diet. I believe ㉞**those who make an effort will get their just deserts**.

Georgie: Did you say dessert? Yes, please!

NOTES

☐ **diet** 食事・食生活
  例 **follow a healthy diet** 健康的な食事をする
  I'm on a diet. ダイエット中
  I'm going to go on a diet. ダイエットするつもり

☐ **those who** Ⓢ + Ⓥ SがVする人々 参 **those** は **people** と言い換えられる
  例 **Heaven helps those who help themselves.** 天は自ら助くる者を助く

関係代名詞

TRANSLATION

ブラウン家はホテルで朝食をとっています。

Emily: ジョージー、そんなにコロッケを食べるんじゃないわ！
Georgie: だって、美味しいんだもの！
Angela: エミリーの言う通りよ。おばあさんはいつも「人間は食べるもので決まる」ってよく言っていたわよ。
Trevor: そうだね、君は元気だよね、アンジェラ。お義母さんの言っていたことが証明されたね。
Angela: そうよ、いつも健康的な食生活をしようと努力しているのよ。努力する人はふさわしい結果が得られると思うわ。
Georgie: "デザート"って言った？　はい、お願いします。

WORDS & EXPRESSIONS

- **croquette** 名 コロッケ　※もとはフランス語
- **dear** 名 あなた　愛する人への呼びかけ
- **be in great shape** 申し分のない状態、体調が良い
  - 反 be under the weather　元気がない（既出）
- **turn out** （結果）〜になる
- **get one's just deserts** ふさわしい結果を得る
  - ※ desert は dessert と発音は同じだが、意味は「砂漠」。just deserts のように複数形で「当然の結果、報い」
- **dessert** 名 デザート

Exploring Grammar

注意すべき「先行詞を含む関係代名詞 what」

● what は先行詞を含む関係代名詞。

You are what you eat.
あなたは食べるもので決まる

You are what you read.
読書があなたを決める

You are what you think.
行動を見れば、その人の考えが分かる

コマーシャルなどでは、

You are what you buy.
買うものであなたの人生（人柄）が決まる

などとあおる。

I owe what I am today to my father.
私が現在あるのは父のおかげだ

Obihiro is no longer what it used to be when I lived there.
帯広市はもはや私が住んでいたころとは違っている

その他注意すべき関係代名詞の用法

- 先行詞が"もの"でも"人"でも所有格は whose を用いる。

**I want to buy the book + Its cover is full of pictures.
= I want to buy the book whose cover is full of pictures.**
表紙が写真でいっぱいのその本を買いたい

- 先行詞が"もの"の場合は whose の代わりに of which を使うことが可能。

I want to buy the book the cover of which is full of pictures. = I want to buy the book of which the cover is full of pictures.

- "人"の例：

Taro is a young actor. + Taro's father used to be an actor, too. = Taro is a young actor whose father used to be one (an actor), too.
太郎は若い俳優ですがお父さんも俳優でした

- 先行詞に"最上級"や the very、the first、the only など強い限定の意味を持つ修飾語がついた場合や、先行詞に all、every、any、no などがついた場合は関係代名詞は that を用いる。

This is the best movie that I have ever seen in my life.
これはこれまで見た中で最高の映画だ

He is the first astronaut that took a ride in a spaceship.
彼は宇宙船に乗った最初の宇宙飛行士だ

You can choose any book that you are interested in for reading.
読書のためには興味があるどんな本を選んでもよい

- 先行詞が人と動物などの場合も that を用いる。

  Take a look at that boy and his dog that are trying to swim in the river.
  川で泳ごうとしている少年と犬を見てごらん

- 関係代名詞が be 動詞の補語の働きをする場合には that を用いる。

  Jack is no longer the honest man (that) he once was.
  彼はもはや以前の正直な男ではない

- 前文の内容を受け継ぐ非制限用法の which がある。

  He said he had witnessed the murder that night, which proved to be a lie.
  彼はその夜殺人を目撃したと言った、しかしそれは嘘だとわかった

  Mr. Lia spoke well of one of his students, which made other students jealous.
  リア先生は一人の学生を褒めた、そのことが他の学生にやきもちを焼かせた

STRATEGIES FOR THE TOEIC

CAN YOU REMEMBER...?

- **Fill the blanks with the correct relative pronoun.**

  | that / which / what / whose |

  1 You are _____ you eat.

2 I want to buy the book _____ cover is full of pictures.

3 He said he witnessed the murder that night, _____ proved to be a lie.

4 This is the best movie _____ I have ever seen in my life.

5 He is the first astronaut _____ took a ride in a spaceship.

6 I owe _____ I am today to my father

CAN YOU GUESS...?

• **Fill the blanks with a relative pronoun.**

7 The sports car _____ is parked outside my house belongs to my dad.

8 Mariko came to visit yesterday, _____ was a pleasant surprise!

9 She was wearing some trendy shoes _____ laces were multi-colored!

10 Bill told me he got divorced last week, _____ came as a big shock to me.

ANSWERS

1 what   **2** whose   **3** which   **4** that   **5** that   **6** what
7 that / which   **8** which   **9** whose   **10** which

Review 2

Fill the blanks. Use the words in brackets ( ) to help you.
If the words are separated by a slash (/), choose the correct word or words.

🗝 Grammar Keys ⑲ ~ ㉔

A. I think he _____ (can't / must) be sick. He has such a small appetite.

B. He _____ (might get) food poisoning from the raw fish we had yesterday.

C. Wow! Who's that? Is that your _____?
(boy friend / boy-friend / boyfriend)

D. Why don't we go into town this weekend and buy _____ (a furniture / some furniture / some furnitures) for our new apartment?

E. I _____ my hair _____ (have cut) yesterday.

F. I'll get the engine _____ (go). We have a long drive ahead.

Grammar Keys 25 ~ 30

G. The house next door is still _____ (build). It's so noisy!

H. Japanese houses _____ (make) of wood and paper.

I. I'm really _____ (look forward) to _____ (see) my grandma in the holidays. I've been _____ it _____ (put off) for too long.

J. I work _____ a small computer company _____ London, established almost twenty years ago _____ my father. (on / by / for / to / in)

K. I guess _____ (some / none / all) class reunions are fun while _____ (another / other / others) are terrible.

L. _____ (Me / My / Mine) friends are reliable, while _____ (you / your / yours) are unreliable.

Grammar Keys 31 ~ 34

M. Can you _____ (make / a / do / the / me / you) favor? Can you help me carry this bag to my room?

N. How _____ (many / much) does it weigh? 100 kilograms?

Review 2

O. _____ you already _____ (have – negative question) a million books in your room? You _____ more, _____? (need – negative tag question)

P. Another bag? How _____ (many / much) bags have you got?

Q. _____ (What / That / Which) your mom said turns out to be true.

R. I've always tried hard to follow a healthy diet. I believe _____ who make an effort will get _____ just deserts. (their / these / they / those)

Answer Key

A. I think he <u>must</u> be sick.

B. He <u>might have got (gotten)</u> food poisoning from the raw fish we had yesterday.

C. Is that your <u>boyfriend</u>?

D. Why don't we go into town this weekend and buy <u>some furniture</u> for our new apartment?

E. I <u>had</u> my hair <u>cut</u> yesterday.

F. I'll get the engine <u>going</u>.

G. The house next door is still <u>being built</u>.

H. Japanese houses <u>are made</u> of wood and paper.

I. I'm really <u>looking forward</u> to <u>seeing</u> my grandma in the holidays. I've been <u>putting</u> it <u>off</u> for too long.

J. I work <u>for</u> a small computer company <u>in</u> London, established almost twenty years ago <u>by</u> my father.

K. I guess <u>some</u> class reunions are fun, while <u>others</u> are terrible.

L. <u>My</u> friends are reliable, while <u>yours</u> are unreliable.

M. Can you <u>do me a</u> favor?

N. How <u>much</u> does it weigh?

O. <u>Don't</u> you already <u>have</u> a million books in your room? You <u>don't need</u> more, <u>do you</u>?

P. How <u>many</u> bags have you got?

Q. <u>What</u> your mom said turns out to be true.

R. I believe <u>those</u> who make an effort will get <u>their</u> just deserts.

UNIT 21 Reported speech

㉟ **Questions**…疑問文　㊱ **Say and tell**…伝達動詞
㊲ **Think**…伝達動詞

LISTEN & READ

John and Keiko are thinking of renovating their new apartment.

John: I spoke with the architect today. ㉟**I asked him how much it would cost** to renovate our apartment. ㊱**He said he would look into it and let me know.**

Keiko: Well, ㊱**my dad told me that it would cost an arm and a leg.** ㉟**He asked me why we were renovating a new apartment.**

John: What? ㊲**I thought *you* wanted to renovate the place.**

Keiko: No. ㊲**I thought *you* did!** ㊱**You told me that there wasn't enough space for your desk** and ㊱**you said you needed a bigger office!**

John: Mm. I guess it might be cheaper just to get a smaller desk then!

NOTES

☐ **reform**　日本語で言う「リフォーム」は英語では「政治改革」や「信条の変更」などを意味し住居などには用いない。一般には **renovate**「（古い建物・部屋・家具などを）修理・改装・復元する」を用いる。その他 **redecorate** は「（カーテンやじゅうたんなどの）変更」など簡単なもの、**rebuild** は「家などを（更地に戻すなどして）建て替える」大改修の場合に用いる。

☐ **I guess**　同＝ I think

間接疑問文

TRANSLATION

ジョンと恵子は新しいアパートをリフォームしようかと考えています。

- John: 今日建築業者と話したよ。アパートをリフォームするのにいくらかかるのか聞いたよ。調べて連絡すると言っていた。
- Keiko: そうね、父はかなりお金がかかるよって言ってたわ。新しいアパートをどうしてリフォームするのかって聞いてたわ。
- John: どうしてだって？ 君がアパートをリフォームしたがっていると思っていたよ。
- Keiko: 違うわ。あなたが望んでると思ってたわ！ デスクのためのスペースが足りない、もっと広いオフィスが欲しいって言ってたでしょ。
- John: うーん。小さいデスクを買う方が安上がりのようだね！

WORDS & EXPRESSIONS

- ☐ **architect** 名 建築家・建築業者
- ☐ **look into (sth)** 〜を調査する、調べる
- ☐ **let + 人 + know** 〜に知らせる、連絡する
- ☐ **cost an arm and a leg** 大金がかかる
  - 参 cost a large amount of money の比喩。

Exploring grammar

疑問文を伝える：間接疑問文の作り方

● 2つの文から間接疑問文を作るときの注意点

How much will it cost to have my camera repaired?
カメラを修理してもらうのにいくらかかりますか

I asked the repairman. 修理屋さんに聞いた

1文にすると……
↓

I asked the repairman how much it would cost to have my camera repaired.

☞ How much will it ～の部分を、〈S＋V〉の語順にして、will を asked の時制に合わせて、過去形にする（時制の一致）ことに注意。

● 直接疑問文を間接疑問文にするときの注意点

He said to me, "Why are you so mad?"
彼は「どうしてそんなに怒っているの」と私に言った

この文を間接疑問文にするとき、疑問文を伝えるので said to を"尋ねた"の asked に変えて He asked me として、疑問詞 why でそのままつなげて〈S＋V〉の語順にすると、

He asked me why I was so mad.
となる。

I said to her. と疑問詞のない Do you want to go out with me? を1文にする際には時制だけでなく、代名詞の変更にも気をつける。伝達動詞は said to を asked に変える。疑問詞がないので、「～かどうか」を表すため、if か whether でつなげて、

I asked her if she wanted to go out with me.
私は彼女に交際する気があるかどうか聞いた

となる。

平叙文を伝える

I thought　私は思った

It will cost a lot of money to have my camera repaired.
カメラを修理してもらうのに多額のお金がかかるだろう

１文にすると……
↓

I thought it would cost a lot of money to have my camera repaired.

☞ will → would の時制の一致に気をつけるだけでよい。

He said to me.　彼は私に言った

There is no time to lose.　無駄にできる時間はない

１文にすると……
↓

He told me (that) there was no time to lose.

☞ said to を told に変えることと時制に注意。

● Dialogue の Keiko の１回目と John そして Keiko の２回目を２文に分けてみよう。

Keiko: **Well, my dad said to me, "It will cost an arm and a leg." He said to me, "Why are we renovating a new apartment?"**

John: **What? I thought + 'You want to renovate the place.'**

Keiko: **No. I thought + 'You want (to renovate the place).' You said to me, "There isn't enough space for my desk and I need a bigger office."**

となる。

その他の注意点

- 命令文は"命令"か"依頼"かを区別して動詞を tell「～しろと言う」か〈ask「～してください」＋目的語＋to 不定詞〉の構文にする。

    I said to my mom, "Please wait for me here."
    = I asked my mom to wait for me there.
    ママに、「ここで私を待っていてください」と言った

- 否定の命令の場合は not to 不定詞で「～しないように」を表す。

    He also said to us, "Don't bother other people around you."
    = He also told us not to bother other people around us.
    先生は「周りの人たちに迷惑をかけないように」と言った

- 時や場所を表す語（句）は状況に合わせて変更する。

    Our teacher said to us, "Keep quiet now."
    = Our teacher told us to keep quiet then.
    先生は「今は静かにしていなさい」と私たちに言った

    ☛ now が then に変わることに注意。

STRATEGIES FOR THE TOEIC

CAN YOU REMEMBER...?

- For questions 1 ~ 4, change each sentence into reported speech.

1 How much will it cost to have my camera repaired?

I asked the repairman _____
_____.

2 Why are you so mad?

He asked me _____
_____.

3 Do you want to go out with me?

I asked her _____

_____ .

4 I said to my mom, "Please wait for me here?"

I asked _____

_____ .

- **For questions 5 and 6, choose the correct verb.**

5 Well, my dad _____ to me, "It will cost an arm and a leg." (said / told)

6 He also _____ us not to bother other people around us. (said / told)

CAN YOU GUESS...?

- **Rewrite the jumbled sentences in the correct order.**

7 I he me him asked loved if

_____ .

8 me that didn't sushi he he told like

_____ .

9 were I Japan you thought from

_____ .

10 asked moved he why Boston to me I

_____ .

ANSWERS

1 how much it would cost to have my camera repaired **2** why I was so mad **3** if she wanted to go out with me **4** my mom to wait for me there. **5** said **6** told **7** I asked him if he loved me **8** He told me that he didn't like sushi **9** I thought you were from Japan **10** He asked me why I moved to Boston

UNIT 22 Subjunctives

  ㊳ Subjunctives…仮定法

LISTEN & READ

Maki has just passed her driver's test.

Maki: I'm so happy I passed my driver's test! I'm really grateful to you, Kate. **㊳Had it not been for your help and support, I wouldn't have passed.**

Kate: Nonsense! I didn't do anything. **㊳Were it not for your hard work and patience, you might not have passed first time.**

Maki: **㊳I wish I were rich. Then I'd buy a brand new car today!** Oh, **㊳if only I had a rich boyfriend, then he could buy me a sports car!**

Kate: I think that's wishful thinking, Maki! **㊳I wish you would get your head out of the clouds.** You'll have to settle for a cheap used car for now!

Maki: Mm. I guess you're right, but there's no harm in dreaming, is there?

NOTES

☐ **That's wishful thinking.**　それは甘い考えだ、希望的観測だよ　`人をたしなめる表現`

☐ **get one's head out of the clouds**　現実を直視する　`慣用表現`
　例 **Get your head out of the clouds.**　いつまで夢みたいなことを考えてるんだ

仮定法

TRANSLATION

麻紀は運転免許試験に受かったばかりです。

Maki: 運転免許がとれてすごく嬉しいわ！　本当にあなたに感謝ね、ケイト。あなたの援助がなければ受からなかったと思うわ。

Kate: とんでもない。私は何もしていないわ。あなたの努力と忍耐がなければ1回で受からなかったかもしれないわ。

Maki: お金持ちならいいのにな、だったら今日にでも新車を買うのにね。それともリッチなボーイフレンドがいれば、スポーツカーを買ってくれるかもね。

Kate: 麻紀、考えが甘いわよ！　現実を直視してもらいたいわ。今は安い中古車に落ち着かなくてはね。

Maki: うん。あなたの言う通りね、でも夢見るだけなら害はないでしょ。

WORDS & EXPRESSIONS

- **driver's test**　運転免許試験
- **I'm really grateful to you.**　本当にありがたいと思っている
  - grateful ＝ thankful
- **Nonsense!**　とんでもない、バカなことを言わないで
- **patience**　名 忍耐力　参 **patient**　形 辛抱強い、名 患者
- **brand new**　まっさらの
- **wishful thinking**　希望的観測、甘い考え
- **settle for**　（不満足ながらも）〜でよしとする、〜という結果を甘んじて受ける
- **harm**　名 損害・悪意

EXPLORING GRAMMAR

仮定法の注意点

一般的な条件文や仮定法の基本は Unit 5 に記述したので、ここでは "仮定法の特別な用法" について述べる。

● "倒置"（主語と動詞の語順が入れ替わると理解してよい）で "条件" を表す。

この構文に用いられる助動詞、be 動詞は **were**、**had**、**should** に限られる。"仮定法過去形" の文である。

If I were a bird, I could fly to you.
もし鳥だったらあなたのもとへ飛んでいけるのに

☛ If を省略して、Were I a bird, I could fly to you.（Were I の部分が "倒置"）としても同じ意味を表す。ただし文語の響きになる。"過去に関する仮定" を表す "仮定法過去完了形" の文でも同様にできる。

If the mayor had supported the candidate, he could have won the election over the opponent.
もし市長がその候補者を支援していたら、彼はその選挙で対立候補に勝てただろう

If を略して……
↓

Had the mayor supported the candidate, he could have won the election over his opponent.

☛ Had the mayor と倒置することによって仮定法過去完了形となる。

● この形を用いることが多い慣用的な文には

Were it not for her aid, I could not go on with my project.
彼女の援助がなければ、プロジェクトを続けられないだろう（現在についての仮定）

"過去" のことを述べるなら……
↓

Had it not been for the financial support from the government, they could not have established the new NPO.
政府からの援助がなければ、彼らは新しいNPOを設立できなかっただろう

- いずれの文も But for ～、Without ～を用いて同じ意味を単文（〈S + V〉の組み合わせが文中に1組）で表せる。

But for / Without her aid, I could not go on with my project. But for / Without the financial support…

- 応用編として次の各文の意味を考えてみよう。

Were it not for modern technology, we could not live a convenient life as we do now.
現代の科学技術がなければ、今のような便利な生活は送れないだろう

Had he known that she already had a fiancé, he would not have asked her out.
彼女に婚約者がいると知っていたら、彼は彼女をデートに誘ったりしなかったのに

Should the man come again, what should I tell him? (= If the man should come again,…)
万が一あの男がもう一度来たら、何と言うべきでしょうか
☞ この文の should は "仮定法で可能性がほとんどないこと" を仮定するときに用いる。意味は「万が一～したら」のようにするとニュアンスが伝わる。

If only、Would that で I wish の意味を伝える

If only my father were alive! We were so dependent on him.
父が生きていてくれさえすればいいのに！　すごく頼っていたのよ

Would that we could see him again!
もう一度彼に会えればいいのに

It's time / It's about time の構文

It's time you started to get to work.
もう仕事に取りかかる時間だよ

It's about time　そろそろ〜する時間だ　※意味を和らげる。

It's high time　すぐにでも〜する時間だ　※意味を強める。

It's about time young kids went to bed.　子供は寝る時間だ！

It's high time we apologized to our parents.
すぐにでも両親に謝るべきときだ

☛ これらの構文では動詞（went, apologized）を仮定法過去形にして"まだしていないこと"に対する"切迫"感を表している。

as if / as though で「まるで〜のように」を表す

● as if, as though は全く同じ意味を表す。

Taro is not our teacher, but he acts as if / though he were our teacher.
太郎は先生でもないのに、まるで先生のように振る舞うのよ

My father speaks as if / though he knew everything about the business world.
父はその業界のことは何でも知っているような口ぶりだ

☛ これらの文は"現在の事実に反する仮定"を表すので、仮定法過去形を使う。

He talks about Italy as if / though he had been there himself.
彼はまるで自分がイタリアに行った経験があるかのようにイタリアの話をする

Mom looked pale as if / though she had seen a ghost.
ママは幽霊でも見たかのように蒼ざめていた

☛ この文では"過去または現在までの経験"を表すので、仮定法過去完了形を用いる。

Strategies for the TOEIC

Can you remember...?

• **Fill the blanks with words from this unit.**

1. If I _____ a bird, I could fly to you.
2. _____ it not for her aid, I _____ not go on with my project.
3. _____ he known that she already had a fiancé, he would not _____ asked her out.
4. It's _____ time young kids _____ to bed.
5. It's time you (start / starting / started) to get to work.
6. Mom looked pale _____ she _____ a ghost.

Can you guess...?

• **Fill the blanks. Use the verbs in brackets.**

7. If I _____ rich, I _____ a house in Beverly Hills. (buy)
8. It's _____ time you _____ a job. (find)
9. _____ it not _____ for your help, I wouldn't have succeeded. (be)
10. If only he _____ a helmet, then he wouldn't _____ in hospital. (wear, end up)

Answers

1. were 2. Were, could 3. Had, have 4. about / high, went
5. started 6. as if / as though, had seen 7. were, would buy / could buy
8. high / about, found 9. Had, been 10. had worn / had been wearing, have ended up

UNIT 23 Tenses (1)

㊴ Past simple and past continuous…単純過去形と過去進行形

LISTEN & READ

John gets home from work to find that Keiko has a headache.

John: I'm home! Hello! Keiko, are you home?

Keiko: Oh, I'm sorry, ㊴**I was taking a nap when you came in.** I didn't hear you.

John: Are you OK? You look a little pale.

Keiko: ㊴**After I finished work, I had a headache and I was feeling chilly.** I might be coming down with a cold.

John: That's too bad. Now, you stay in bed and I'll fix you a hot lemon drink.

Keiko: Oh, thank you honey! That's so sweet of you!

NOTES

☐ **I didn't hear you.** （ただいまという声が）聞こえなかった

☐ **You look pale.** 顔色が悪い（青い）

☐ 体調を表すのに **have** が便利：
have a headache「頭痛がする」、**have a stomachache**「おなか（胃）が痛い」、**have a fever**「熱がある」、**have the flu**「インフルエンザにかかっている」、**have a sore throat**「のどが痛い」、**have stiff shoulders**「肩が凝っている」、**have a bad tooth**「虫歯がある」、**have indigestion**「消化不良を起こしている」、**have diarrhea**「下痢をしている」など **have** を用いる表現が多い。
※病気ではないが have a hangover といえば「二日酔いだ」となる。

☐ **come down with** （病気に）かかる、（病で）倒れる
例 **I feel like I am coming down with the flu.**
　どうやらインフルエンザをひきかけているようだ

☐ **It's (That's) so sweet of you!** 優しいのね
※意味上の主語 (you) の性格・性質を褒めたり、けなしたりする場合は意味上の主語の前に **for** ではなくて、**of** を用いる。
例 **It's silly of me to trust such a man.** あんな人を信じるなんてバカだったわ

時制 (1)

TRANSLATION

ジョンが仕事から帰宅すると恵子は頭痛がしていました。

John: ただいま！　恵子、帰っているかい？

Keiko: ごめんなさい。あなたが帰宅したとき、うたた寝をしていたの。聞こえなかったの。

John: 大丈夫かい？　ちょっと顔色が悪いようだよ。

Keiko: 仕事が終わった後、頭痛がして寒気がしたの。風邪をひきかけているのかもしれないわ。

John: それは気の毒に。じゃあ、君は横になっていて、僕がホットレモンを作るから。

Keiko: まあ、ありがとう、あなた！　優しいのね！

WORDS & EXPRESSIONS

- **nap** 名昼寝　**take a nap** 昼寝をする　※ take を用いることに注意。
- **pale** 形蒼白な、顔色が悪い
- **chilly** 形寒気がする、冷え冷えする
- **That's too bad.** それは気の毒に
- **fix (a drink)** 動(飲み物を)準備する、作る

EXPLORING GRAMMAR

過去形と過去進行形

- 過去時制の用法：過去の特定の時期に行われた動作を表す。

  I met him last week. 先週彼に会った

  World War II broke out in 1939.
  第二次世界大戦は1939年に勃発した

  ☛ いずれも過去の特定の時期が明示されている。前後関係で自明のときもある。

  Our plane landed 20 minutes ahead of schedule.
  我々の（乗った）飛行機は予定より20分早く着陸した

  I bought this camera in Germany. このカメラはドイツで買った

- 過去時制を用いることで、"現在はそうではない" ことも表せる。

  I taught English in Hamamatsu for 19 years (but I do not teach English, or I do not teach there now).
  浜松で19年間英語を教えていました
  （今は英語を教えていないか、浜松では教えていない）

  That photographer lived and worked in New York for a long time (but he does not live and work there now).
  あの写真家は長い間ニューヨークに住み仕事をしていた
  （今はニューヨークに住んで仕事をしていない）

  上の文を現在完了の文と比べると……
  ↓
  He has lived and worked in New York for 20 years now.
  彼は20年間ニューヨークに住んで仕事をしている（今も）

- 過去時制の用法：過去の習慣を表す。

    She always carried her smartphone wherever she went.
    彼女はどこに行くにもスマホを常に携帯していた

    My parents never drank wine.
    両親は決してワインは口にしなかった

    ☛ たいてい"頻度を表す副詞"とともに使う。

- "頻繁に行われた行為"には would を用い、"長期にわたる習慣"には used to を用いて区別する。

    My father would often return home drunk.
    父はしばしば酔って帰宅したものだ

    My son is much better off than he used to be.
    息子は以前に比べると裕福だ

    ☛ この文の場合 was を用いてもよいが、"長期にわたる"ニュアンスは used to be の方がよく表せる。

- 現在進行形と同じく、always などとともに"常習的行為"を表せる。

    One of my colleagues was always finding fault with me.
    同僚の一人は何かというと私に難癖をつけていた

- 過去のある期間に続いていた動作は過去進行形で表す（いつ始まっていつ終わったのかは明示されない）。

    I'm sorry I was taking a bath when you gave me a ring.
    君が電話をくれたときにはお風呂に入っていたんだよ、ごめんね
    ☛ "電話をしてきた"時点での"進行中の動作"を表している。

    What were you doing when the movie was playing on TV?
    テレビでその映画をやっていたときには何をしていたんだい

- 時を特定せずに

    It was getting darker and darker.
    どんどん暗くなっていた

    The rain was letting up. 雨は上がるところだった

- ある時を示して、その時点の前に始まり、おそらくその時点の後も続いていたと思われる動作も表す。

    At seven thirty we were having dinner.
    7時半には夕食を食べていました
    ☛ 従って7時半には食事が途中であったことが知れる。

    これを過去時制で表現すると……
    ↓
    At seven thirty we had dinner.
    7時半に夕食を食べました
    ☛ "7時半の時点"で「食事を始めたか、食べ終えた」となる。

- 現在進行形が(近接)未来を表すのと同様に、過去進行形が"その時に近かった未来"を表す。

    Our students were busy packing, for they were leaving for the next place that night.
    学生たちはその夜次の場所に出発するため、荷造りに忙しかった

STRATEGIES FOR THE TOEIC

CAN YOU REMEMBER...?

- **Fill the blanks. Use the words in brackets.**

1 I'm sorry I _____ a bath when you _____ me a ring.   (take, give)

2 World War II _____ in 1939. (break out)

3 My father _____ often _____ home drunk.
(return)

4 What _____ you _____ when the movie _____ on TV? (do, play)

5 I _____ this camera in Germany. (buy)

6 I _____ him last week. (meet)

CAN YOU GUESS...?

- **Fill the blanks with a past form of the verbs in brackets.**

7 The squirrel _____ a nut when it _____ out of the tree. (eat, fall)

8 When the plane _____, it _____.
(land, snow)

9 While I _____ TV, the earthquake _____. (watch, strike)

10 What _____ you _____ when she _____ home? _____? (do, come, sleep)

Answers

1 was taking, gave **2** broke out **3** would, return **4** were, doing, was playing **5** bought **6** met **7** was eating, fell **8** landed, was snowing **9** was watching, struck **10** were, doing, came, Sleeping

UNIT 24 Tenses (2)

🗝 ④⓪ **present perfect continuous** … 現在完了進行形
④① **present perfect simple** … 現在完了形

LISTEN & READ

The Browns are on the Shinkansen leaving for Kyoto. Trevor is sitting next to a Japanese man and strikes up a conversation just before departure.

Passenger: How long ④⓪**have** you **been traveling** in Japan?

Trevor: Almost a week now. ④①We'**ve been** to lots of interesting places, but ④①we **haven't been** to Kyoto yet. Do you live there?

Passenger: Yes. ④①I'**ve lived** in Kyoto for about twenty years.

Trevor: What do you do, if you don't mind my asking?

Passenger: Not at all. I'm a novelist. ④⓪I'**ve been writing** stories since I was a child.

Trevor: Really? ④①**Have** you **had** any books published?

Passenger: Yes. In fact, ④①I'**ve just had** my 5th novel published, so ④⓪I'**ve been attending** a number of book signings here in Tokyo.

Trevor: Cool! Hey, kids, I'm sitting next to a famous writer!

NOTES

☐ **What do you do? = What is your occupation?**　職業は何ですか

☐ **if you don't mind my asking**　もし差し支えなかったら
　※相手の気持ちを聞く表現。喜んで答える場合は、「ちっとも気にしない」という意味で、No, not at all. と否定を用いる。
　参 答えるのが嫌なときは、**I'm sorry I do**「申し訳ないですが、ダメです」と言う。

☐ **have a book published**　本を出版する
　参 〈have＋目的語＋過去分詞〉の構文

時制 (2)

TRANSLATION

ブラウン家の人たちは京都行きの新幹線に乗っています。トレバーは日本人の男性の隣に座っています。出発の直前に会話を始めます。

Passenger: どれくらい日本を旅行しているのですか？

Trevor: ほぼ1週間ですね。多くの興味深いところには行ったことがあるのですが、まだ京都には行ったことがないのですよ。京都に住んでいるのですか？

Passenger: ええ。もうおよそ20年住んでいますね。

Trevor: 差し支えなければ、お仕事は何をなさっていますか？

Passenger: 構いませんよ。小説家なんです。子供のころからずっと書いていますよ。

Trevor: 本当ですか？ 出版されたものもあるのですか？

Passenger: はい。実は、ちょうど5冊目が出版されたので、東京でのいくつかのサイン会に出ているのですよ。

Trevor: カッコいいですね！ ねえ、子供たち、有名な作家さんの隣に座っているんだよ！

WORDS & EXPRESSIONS

- **strike up a conversation = begin a conversation**　会話を始める
- **novelist**　名 小説家
- **publish**　動 出版する・(本などを) 出す
- **a number of**　いくつかの〜・多くの〜
  ※はっきりと"多数"を述べる場合は a large number of を用いる。
- **book signing**　本のサイン会
- **Cool!**　カッコいい・すごい
- **famous**　形 有名な
  ※「無名な」は unknown を使う。infamous は「悪名高い」「評判が悪い」となるので要注意。

Exploring Grammar

現在完了形の表す意味と用法

● 現在完了形は"現在と過去"の結びつきを重んじて"完了""継続""経験"そして"結果"を表す。

完了したばかりの動作：

Mom has just gone out. (=Mom went out a moment ago.)
ママはたった今出かけたところです
☛ 〈has just＋過去分詞〉で表し、主に肯定文や疑問文で使われる。

Has she gone out? 今でかけたばかりですか
☛ 否定文では用いられない。

"Have you had lunch yet?" "Yes, I have already had it."
朝食はおすみですか？ はい、もうすませました
☛ はっきりとは述べていないが"近い過去"に"完了"したことを示している。過去時制のところでも述べたが、"Yes, I had it at seven."と言えば時間がはっきりとすることになる。

この現在完了形の質問に対しては、現在完了形で答えるが、過去を明示する副詞を伝えたい場合は"過去時制"を用いる。単に"完了"したことなら"現在完了形"がふさわしい。

● 次の2つの文の違いを考えてみよう。

1. Jack has sent me five e-mails this morning already.
（まだお昼前くらいの発言）ジャックったら朝だけでもう5通もメールを送ってきたの

2. Jack sent me five e-mails this morning.
（おそらく午後になってからの発言）ジャックは午前中に5通メールを送ってきた
☛ this afternoon もおよそ17時くらいまでを指すので、this morning と同じように"現在完了形"と"過去形"が共存すると言える。

Have you seen Steve today? 今日スティーブに会ったかい
☛ at any time today を表す。

Have you seen Steve lately / recently?
最近スティーブに会ったかい
☛ lately / recently は話者の意識ではまだ終了していない時間の範囲を述べている。

He hasn't been around here lately / recently.
彼は近ごろこのあたりには近づいていないよ

いつであるかは明示せず、過去に行った経験：

One of my students says she has seen the movie, Frozen, more than six times.
『アナと雪の女王』を6回以上見たと言っている学生がいます

I have lived downtown. ダウンタウンに住んだことがあります

かなり古い経験でもこれで表現：

Have you ever seen a wild urchin?
天然のウニを見たことがありますか

Yes, many times. はい何度でもありますよ
☛ ever を添えることで "これまでの人生のいつでもいいから" の意味を持つ。

「〜に行った経験」はこの構文では必須：

Have you ever been to the zoo?
動物園には行ったことがありますか

I have been to Ueno Zoo more than five times.
上野動物園には5回以上行ったことがあります

This is the best whiskey I have ever drunk.
これまで飲んだ中で最高のウイスキーだ

This is the only novel she has written.
彼女が書いた小説はこれだけです

動作の結果が現在どのようになっているか：

Barry has had a bad car accident. (Probably he is still in the hospital.)
バリーがひどい交通事故を起こしたんだ（その結果おそらく入院中だ）

My computer has broken down. (So I can't write my essay with it.)
コンピュータが壊れちゃった（だからレポートが書けない）

My mother has cleaned my room. (So there is no dust in my room.)
お母さんが部屋を掃除してしまった（だから部屋にはゴミがない）
　☞ たとえばエッセイの下書きがごみ箱に残っていることを期待している場合などは報われない。

My P.E. teacher has gone ballistic (= got very angry).
体育の先生が激怒した（まだ怒っている）

まだ続いている動作：

I have known him since he was an elementary school pupil.
彼を小学生のころから知っている

We have lived in Tokyo for more than 20 years.
東京に２０年以上住んでいる（今も住んでいる）

She has waited for him all day. = she is still waiting.
1日中彼を待っていた

動作の継続：

 know、**live** など"状態"を表す動詞の場合は"現在完了形"で"状態の継続"を表すが、"動作"を表す動詞の場合は"現在完了進行形"で"動作の継続"を表す。

いくつかの動詞は"現在完了形"でも"現在完了進行形"でも用いることができる：

 expect、**hope**、**learn**、**live**、**rain**、**sleep**、**sit**、**stand**、**stay**、**study**、**teach**、**wait**、**want**、**work**　など。

How long have you studied English? / How long have you been studying English?
英語をどのくらいの間勉強していますか

 ☛ まだ"継続"していることを強調するなら have been studying の方が誤解なく伝えられるが、"続けていたが終わったばかり"であれば have studied の方が良いだろう。

"What have you been doing?" "Well, I have been taking photos recently."
「これまで何をしていましたか」「そうですね、最近は写真を撮って（ばかり）います」

That baby has been sleeping for five long hours.
あの赤ちゃんは5時間たっぷり寝ています（まだ寝ていることを強調）

That baby has slept for five hours.
あの赤ちゃんはもう5時間寝ていました（今は起きていても）

STRATEGIES FOR THE TOEIC

CAN YOU REMEMBER...?

- **Use these verbs to fill the blanks.**

sleep / send / see / study / know / have

1. _____ you _____ lunch yet?
2. Jack _____ me five e-mails this morning already.
3. One of my students says she _____ the movie, Frozen, more than six times.
4. That baby _____ for five long hours.
5. I _____ him since he was an elementary school pupil.
6. How long _____ you _____ English?

CAN YOU GUESS...?

- **Complete the conversation using the present perfect simple or the present perfect continuous of the verbs in brackets.**

7 You're covered in grease! What _____ ?
(do)

8 I _____ my car.
(repair)

9 _____ , yet?
(not finish)

10 No. I still _____ the oil.
(not change)

ANSWERS

1 Have, had   **2** has sent   **3** has seen   **4** has been sleeping
5 have known   **6** have, been studying / have, studied   **7** have you been doing   **8** have been repairing   **9** Haven't you finished
10 haven't changed

UNIT 25 Tenses (3)

🔑 **㊷ Present simple – states, habits, routines**
…状態・習慣・型にはまった動作

LISTEN & READ

Sally, a friend of Kate's, stays over at Kate and Maki's apartment. The next morning, Kate is in the kitchen preparing breakfast.

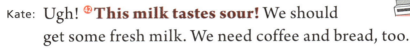

Kate: Ugh! ㊷ **This milk tastes sour!** We should get some fresh milk. We need coffee and bread, too.

Maki: I'll go to Family Market. ㊷ **They sell milk at a low price** in that store.

Sally: Morning, Kate.

Kate: Morning, Sally. Did you sleep well?

Sally: Like a baby, thanks. ㊷ **I usually get up earlier, around 6,** but it was so warm in that cozy bed! Where's Maki?

Kate: She's gone shopping for fresh milk. ㊷ **We take turns shopping and cooking breakfast.** What'll you have? Fish, rice, natto?

Sally: Er, no thanks. ㊷ **I usually just have coffee and toast.** I'll give the natto a miss, thanks!

NOTES

- **This milk tastes sour.**　ミルクが酸っぱい（腐っている）
  参 taste は「〜という味がする」と状態を表す動詞。

- **sleep like a baby**　ぐっすりと眠る
  同 **sleep like a log**　（丸太のように）ぐっすり眠る

- **give ~ a miss**　〜をパスする・〜はやめておく・〜を欠席する 慣用表現

時制 (3)

TRANSLATION

ケイトの友達のサリーはケイトと麻紀のアパートに泊まりに来ます。翌朝ケイトは台所で朝食のしたくをしています。

Kate: うわっ！　このミルク酸っぱいわ（腐っているわ）。新しいのを買わなきゃ。コーヒーとパンも必要ね。

Maki: ファミリーマーケットに行ってくるわ。あの店では牛乳が安いのよ。

Sally: おはよう、ケイト。

Kate: おはよう、サリー。よく眠れた？

Sally: ぐっすり眠れたわ、ありがとう。たいていはもっと朝早く、6時くらいに起きるのだけど、寝心地がよい温かいベッドだったから！　麻紀はどこに行ったの？

Kate: ミルクを買いに行ったわ。交代で買い物と朝食作りをしているの。何を食べる？　魚、ご飯、納豆？

Sally: あー、結構よ。たいていコーヒーとトーストだけよ。ありがとう、納豆はパスするわ！

WORDS & EXPRESSIONS

- **Ugh!**　うわっ　※驚きや不快を表す。
- **Morning! (Good morning!)**　おはよう　※Good を略すことが多い。
- **cozy**　形 居心地が良い、気が休まる
- **What'll you have?**　何を食べますか

Exploring Grammar

現在形の主な用法

● 習慣的動作を表す。

Babies cry.　赤ん坊は泣くものだ

My father doesn't smoke, but he drinks.
父はタバコは吸わないが、酒は飲みます

現在形（現在時制）との相性の良い副詞（句）：

always、often、sometimes、occasionally、never、every week、on Saturday(s)、three times a month　などがある。

My family goes to church on Sundays.
私の家族は毎週日曜には教会に行きます

In Japan it rains much in June and July.
日本では6月と7月には多くの雨が降ります

Whenever my uncle visits us, he brings something nice.
伯父が家に来るときはいつでも何か素敵なものを持ってきてくれます

The alarm goes off when a fire breaks out.
火事が起きると警報がなります

● 掲示や書籍の記載事項を伝える。

"What does that signboard say?" "It says No Smoking."
「あの看板には何と書いてありますか?」「禁煙と書いてあります」

"You got a letter from Henry. What does he say?" "He says he wants to stay with us."
「ヘンリーから手紙が来たね。何と書いてある?」「うちに泊まりたいと言っているわ」

● 出来事などの進み方を述べる。

Nohmi throws the ball. Abe hits the ball and it goes between the first fielder and the second fielder. The third runner returns home.
能見ボールを投げる。阿部が打ってボールが１塁手と２塁手の間を抜ける。３塁ランナーホームに帰ってくる

Our travel agent; "We leave New York at 10 o'clock this Friday and arrive at Washington D.C. in three hours. We spend about five hours in the Smithsonian National Air and Space Museum. We stay at the Ritz Hotel."
旅行業者；「今週の金曜日の10時にニューヨークを出ます。３時間後にワシントンに到着。スミソニアン国立航空宇宙博物館でおよそ５時間過ごします。リッツホテルに宿泊」

● 不変の真理を表す。

The earth goes round the sun.
地球は太陽の周りをまわっている

A year has 365 days.　１年は365日だ

Three and five make(s) eight.　３＋５は８

Water boils at 100 degrees Celsius.
水は摂氏100度で沸騰する

Time flies like an arrow.　光陰矢の如し（諺）

Time and tide wait for no man.　歳月人を待たず（諺）

The pen is mightier than the sword.　文は武よりも強し（諺）

- 特殊な現在時制

  Here comes the sun!
  ほら朝日が昇ってきたよ（目前の動作を表す表現）

  I hear she is leaving for L.A. next spring.
  彼女は来春ロサンゼルスへ発つそうだ
  (I hear は現在完了形の I have heard の代用と考えられる)

- 時と条件を表す副詞節の中では単純未来は現在形で表す：

  If it is fine tomorrow morning, we will start for the summit.
  明朝晴れたら頂上を目指して出発する予定です

  By the time he comes back, we have to get ready for the surprise party.
  彼が戻ってくるまでに、サプライズパーティーの準備をしなくてはいけない

- 進行形にはしないで現在形で用いる動詞

  This French toast tastes better with more butter.
  このフレンチトーストはバターの量を多くするともっとおいしい

  参 **The sommelier (wine steward) is tasting the new wine.**
  ソムリエが新しいワインを試飲している
  ☛ この「〜を味見する」は進行形にできる。

  This perfume smells gorgeous.
  この香水はゴージャスな香りがする

  参 **The police dog was smelling the rubble for missing people.**
  警察犬は行方不明者を探してがれきの臭いを嗅いでいる
  ☛ taste と同じく他動詞として「〜の臭いを嗅ぐ」として進行形にして使える。

  I know that singer well. あの歌手をよく知っている

知覚に関する動詞は進行形にしない：

notice 気づく　　**see** 見える　　**look** 〜に見える　　など。

嫌悪・好意などの感情を表す動詞も進行形にしない：

admire 感心する　　**appreciate** 感謝する・高く評価する
desire 望む　　**detest** 嫌悪する　　**dislike, hate** 嫌う
fear 恐れる　　**like** 好む　　**mind** 気にする
value 尊重する　　など。

Strategies for the TOEIC

Can you remember...?

- **Fill the blanks. Use the words in brackets.**

1. "You got a letter from Henry. What _____?" "He _____ he wants to stay with us." (say)

2. My father _____, but he _____. (not smoke, drink)

3. The alarm _____ when a fire breaks out. (go off)

- **Commentator;**

4. Abe _____ the ball and it _____ between the first fielder and the second fielder. (hit, go)

- **Our travel agent;**

5. We _____ New York at 10 o'clock this Friday and _____ at Washington D.C. in three hours. (leave, arrive)

6. We _____ about five hours in the Smithsonian National Air and Space Museum. We _____ at the Ritz Hotel. (spend, stay)

CAN YOU GUESS...?

• **Use the following verbs to fill the blanks.**

smell / have / taste / be

7 Pasta _____ better with parmesan cheese.

8 If I _____ time, I'll drive you to the station.

9 Let me check my diary. Sorry. I _____ busy tomorrow, but I _____ free on Tuesday.

10 Mm. That _____ good! I can't wait to taste it!

ANSWERS

1 does he say, says **2** doesn't smoke, drinks **3** goes off
4 hits, goes **5** leave, arrive **6** spend, stay **7** tastes **8** have
9 am, am **10** smells

UNIT 26 Tenses (4)

㊸ Sequence of tenses…時制の一致

LISTEN & READ

John is talking with his business colleague, Makoto, at work.

Makoto: I was surprised when ㊸**the boss said he had been to the United States**.

John: Yes, I met him when he went to New York on business.

Makoto: Really? ㊸**I didn't know that you had lived in New York before moving to Tokyo!**

John: Yes. ㊸**I moved there from L. A. when I joined the company.**

Makoto: I see. So that explains why you and the boss are so chummy!

John: In fact, ㊸**when I met him in New York, he promised he would do his best to find** a position for me here at the Tokyo branch.

NOTES

☐ **go to ~ on business**　～に出張する
　同 = go to ~ on an official errand

☐ 〈**That explains ⓢ + ⓥ**〉　それで～なのが分る
　※直訳では「それ (That) が S が V であることを説明 (explain) している」。
　例 **Well, that explains how you made such a large amount of money.**
　　そうだね、それで君が大金を稼いだ方法が分かるよ

時制 (4)

TRANSLATION

ジョンは職場の同僚の誠と話をしています。

Makoto: ボスがアメリカに行ったことがあるって言ったときは驚いたよ。

John: そうだよ、彼がニューヨークに出張したときに会ったんだよ。

Makoto: そうかい？　君が東京に引っ越す前にニューヨークに住んでいたなんて知らなかったよ！

John: そうだよ。会社に入ったときにLAから引っ越したんだよ。

Makoto: なるほど。それで君がボスと親しいことがわかったよ！

John: 実は、ニューヨークで会ったときに、僕のために最善を尽くして、東京支店で職を見つけるって約束してくれたんだ。

WORDS & EXPRESSIONS

- [ ] **L. A.**　ロサンゼルス
- [ ] **the company**　（話題になっている）会社
- [ ] **chummy**　形 仲良し・親しい　同 = familiar, intimate
- [ ] **in fact**　実は　参 as a matter of fact とも言う。
- [ ] **do one's best**　最善を尽くす、頑張る
- [ ] **position**　名 職・地位　など
- [ ] **branch**　名 本来は「枝」、会社などでは「支店・支社」

EXPLORING GRAMMAR

時制の一致

● その前に、文の中に主節と従属節があることを復習しておこう。

Everybody knew *that the rumor was not true.*
誰もがその噂は本当でないことを知っていた

The train was delayed *because there was an accident near Machida Station.*
町田駅の近くで事故があったので電車が遅れた

The recession lasted longer *than we had expected.*
景気低迷は予期した以上に長引いた

これらの文で下線部が"主節"で、イタリック体になっている部分が"従属節"である。

時制の一致では、これらの動詞の整合性を求める：

I think (that) it will snow soon. 間もなく雪になるだろうと思う

伝達動詞の think を thought と過去形にすると……
↓
I thought (that) it would snow soon.

と従属節の will も過去形にしなくてはいけない。

She knows (that) her son has committed a crime.
彼女は息子が罪を犯したことを知っている

know を過去形にすると……
↓
She knew (that) her son had committed a crime

（過去完了形）となる。

● 同様の例を挙げておこう。

I think he conveyed the wrong information on the demonstration.
彼はデモに関して間違った情報を伝えたと思う

think を thought にすると……
↓

I thought he had conveyed the wrong information on the demonstration.

少し難しいが……
↓

We have done what we think is inevitable.
我々は不可欠だと思われることをやった

have done を "その時までにした" という had done にすると……
↓

We had done what we thought was inevitable.

となる。

時制の一致は "直接話法" から "間接話法" に変える場合に伝達動詞が過去形の場合にも適用される。Unit 21「間接話法」の項を参照されたい。

● Dialogue の文を "時制の一致" に気をつけて見てみよう。

Makoto: **The boss said he had been to the United States.**

The boss said, "I have been to the United States."
これまでに合衆国に行ったことがある（"経験" を表す "現在完了"）

Makoto: **Really? I didn't know that you had lived in New York before moving to Tokyo!**

I didn't know をとると……
↓
You have lived in New York before moving to Tokyo.
東京に移動する前にはニューヨークにずっと住んでいた
（"継続" を表す "現在完了"）

となる。

John: **Yes. I moved there from L. A. when I joined the company.**
☛ "会社に入った (joined)" と "引っ越した (moved)" が同じ時なので、両方とも過去形。

John: **He promised he would do his best to find a position.**
☛ promised が過去形の伝達動詞になる。

He promised + "I will do my best to find a position."
職を見つけるために最善を尽くすつもりだ
☛ will が would へと "時制の一致" を受けている。

STRATEGIES FOR THE TOEIC

• Fill the blanks. Use the words in brackets ( ).

CAN YOU REMEMBER...?

1. She knew that her son _____ a crime. (commit)
2. The recession lasted longer than we _____. (expect)
3. I thought that it _____ soon. (snow)
4. The train was delayed because there _____ an accident. (be)
5. Everybody knew that the rumor _____ true. (not be)
6. I moved there from L. A. when I _____ the company. (join)

CAN YOU GUESS...?

When I [7] _____ (be) a teacher, I arrived at school one day and when I walked into the classroom, all the students started laughing. I [8] _____ (look down) and I realized that I [9] _____ (leave) home that morning still wearing my house slippers! I [10] _____ (feel) so embarrassed!

ANSWERS

1. had committed 2. had expected 3. would snow 4. had been
5. was not 6. joined 7. was 8. looked down 9. had left
10. felt

UNIT 27　Time expressions (1)

🔑 ㊹ Frequency … 頻度

LISTEN & READ

The Browns are visiting Eiji (a writer Trevor met on the train) for lunch at his home in Kyoto.

Trevor: Thanks for inviting us to your lovely home. Oh, golf clubs! ㊹**How often do you play?**

Eiji: I practice at a golf range ㊹**two or three times a week** and play on a full course **once a month**. Do you play, Trevor?

Trevor: ㊹**Hardly ever.** I can't seem to find the time.

Angela: Yes, Trevor's just too busy. He ㊹**almost never** has time to enjoy himself in England. That's why he took two weeks off and we came to Japan!

Eiji: Then let's go to the golf range after lunch and leave Angela and the kids to chat with my wife!

Trevor: Great idea, Eiji!

NOTES

- **golf club** 「ゴルフ用クラブ（ボールを打つための長い棒）」と「ゴルフクラブ（ゴルフをする人たちの組織や建物）」の両方の意味がある。
- 〈**That's why** Ⓢ + Ⓥ〉　そういうわけで（だから）〜なのだ
  - 例 **Restaurants are crowded on weekends. That's why they refrain from going to one.**　週末はレストランは混んでいる。そういうわけで(だから)彼らは行くのを控える

時間表現 (1)

TRANSLATION

ブラウン家の人たちは（トレバーが新幹線で会った作家の）英治の京都の家にランチをとるために訪れています。

Trevor: 素敵なお家に招いていただいてありがとうございます。おや、ゴルフのクラブですね。何回くらいプレーするんですか？

Eiji: ゴルフ練習場で週に2、3回練習しますね、コースには月に1回くらい出ます。あなたも（ゴルフを）なさるんですか、トレバー？

Trevor: めったにしませんね。時間が見つけられそうにないんですよ。

Angela: そうなんですよ、トレバーは忙しすぎるんです。イギリスでも遊ぶ時間がほとんどとれないんです。だから2週間の休暇をとって日本に来たんです。

Eiji: それでは、ランチの後でゴルフ練習場に行きましょう、奥さんとお子さんたちは私の妻とおしゃべりをしてもらうために残ってもらいましょう！

Trevor: それはいい考えだね、英治。

WORDS & EXPRESSIONS

- ☐ **invite** 名 招待する
- ☐ **lovely** 形 素敵な
- ☐ **practice** 動 練習する
- ☐ **golf range** ゴルフ練習場
- ☐ **a full course** （ゴルフの）フルコース
- ☐ **find the time** （それをするための）時間を見つける
- ☐ **take (time) off** （休暇を）とる
- ☐ **chat** 動 おしゃべりをする

EXPLORING GRAMMAR

頻度を表す表現

コミュニケーションを正しく円滑に進めるためには、誤解のないよう覚えておく必要がある。

● 一般的なもの

always いつも　　　　　　**continually** 継続的に、絶えず
frequently 頻繁に　　　　**occasionally** 時折、折にふれて
often しばしば　　　　　　**sometimes** 時々
usually たいていは　　　　**periodically** 定期的に
repeatedly 繰り返し

など

● 使い方の原則

① be 動詞の後に置く、その他の動詞の場合はその前に置く。

My teacher is always on time.
先生はいつも時間を守る

Mom is sometimes particular about what I eat.
ママは私の食べるものに口うるさくなるときがある

My students sometimes come to my class late.
私の学生は時々授業に遅刻する

② しかし、助動詞を伴う場合は最初の助動詞の後に置く。疑問文の時は、〈助動詞＋主語＋副詞〉となる。

My son will never obey what I tell him.
息子は私の言うことに従うためしがない

Though his faults have frequently been pointed out, he ignores it.
頻繁に欠点を指摘されてきているのだが、彼は無視するのだ

- ever（疑問文・否定文・関係代名詞節の中で完了形とともに）、hardly ever（まずめったに～ない）、never, rarely（めったに～ない）、barely（めったに～ない）、scarcely ever, seldom など "否定を含む" 副詞

Have you ever been abroad?
（これまでに）海外に行ったことがありますか

No, this is the first time that I have ever visited a foreign country.
いいえ、外国を訪れるのは今回が初めてです

He hardly ever goes fishing with his colleagues.
彼はまずめったに同僚と釣りに行かない

Tim almost never replies to my e-mails.
ティムはまず私のメールに返信してこない

His family almost never dine out on weekends.
彼の家族は週末はほとんど外食はしない

Two of a trade seldom agree. （諺）
同じ職業の人は気が合わない

How often do you go to the cinema?
どのくらいの頻度で映画に行きますか

上記のような質問に対して、**Almost never.**「まずないね」と否定する場合には主語・動詞を述べず、"単独" でも意味を表す。

- 回数を返事するときには、

Once a week. 週に１回
Three times a month. 月に３回

のように **a + day, week, month, year** などで「～につき」と表現する。

Once in a blue moon. まずめったにないね

というロマンチックな表現もある。
ちなみに "**blue moon**" は「同じ月に満月が２回あるうちの２回目の満月」のことで、「めったにない」となる。

- "否定を含む" 副詞が "強調" のために文頭にくる場合には "倒置" が必要になる。

  Hardly / Scarcely ever did he utter a word without being blamed.
  彼が叱責されないで、言葉を発することはまずなかった＝彼が何か言うと必ず責められた

  Seldom has he agreed with his father.
  彼は父親とは歯車が合ったことがない

- never は肯定の動詞と一緒に使われ「決して（いかなるときも）〜ない」を意味する。

  I have never seen a more amusing movie than this.
  こんなに面白い映画は見たことがない

  Some people never eat meat. 肉を全く食べない人もいます

- 疑問文に never を使って "行われなかった動作に対する驚き" を表すことがある。

  Have you never gone out with any of your girl classmates?
  クラスの女子とデートしたことがないだって

- ever は "（生まれてからの）いつか" の意味を表す。疑問文・否定文に使われることが多い。

  "Hasn't he ever been on a diet?"
  「彼は（これまでに）ダイエットしたことがないのですか」

  "No, he never has." 「はい、一度もありません」

  No one will ever know. 誰にも知られることはないだろう

- 最近の口語では、"原則" を無視した否定文も聞かれる。

  I will never be no teacher no more.
  もうこれ以上先生でいることはないだろう

STRATEGIES FOR THE TOEIC

• **Fill the blanks with words from this unit.**

CAN YOU REMEMBER...?

1. This is the _____ that I have ever visited a foreign country.
2. His family almost _____ dine out on weekends.
3. Two of a trade _____ agree.
4. He _____ ever goes shopping with his mother.
5. No one will _____ know.
6. My teacher is _____ on time.

CAN YOU GUESS...?

7. "Is this the _____ you have visited Japan?" "No. Second."
8. I almost _____ travel abroad. I don't like flying.
9. My mom _____ cooks. In fact, my dad almost _____ even enters the kitchen!
10. "Haven't you _____ been to a pachinko parlor?" "No. Never!"

ANSWERS

1. first time 2. never 3. seldom 4. hardly 5. ever
6. always 7. first time 8. never 9. always, never 10. ever

UNIT 28 Time expressions (2)

- ㊺ since ~　　~以来、for ~　　~の間、~ ago　　~前に
- ㊻ age and time … 年齢と年代

LISTEN & READ

Kate is showing Maki an old family photo album.

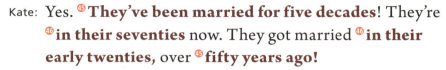

Maki: Are they your grandparents?

Kate: Yes. ㊺**They've been married for five decades**! They're ㊻**in their seventies** now. They got married ㊻**in their early twenties,** over ㊺**fifty years ago!**

Maki: Do you have a picture of your uncle Barry? You often talk about him.

Kate: Actually, ㊺**my real uncle has been dead for 15 years.** Barry isn't really my uncle, but ㊺**I've known him since I was a child.** This is him.

Maki: He looks so young. He must be ㊻**in his 30s.**

Kate: No way! He was born ㊻**in the 1950s,** so he'll be ㊻**in his 60s** now. How time flies!

NOTES

☐ **over / under**　　いずれもその後にくる数字を含まない。
　㊦ **over 50 years old**　　50歳を超えて　　　**under 23**　　23歳未満
　㋹ **Under 18 No Tobacco. We Card. Please Have ID Ready.**
　　18歳未満にはたばこを売りません。チェックします。身分証明書をご用意

☐ **No way!**　　いやいや・それはない！　　※返事として「それは嫌だ」「ありえない」もある。

時間表現 (2)

TRANSLATION

ケイトは麻紀に古い家族アルバムを見せています。

Maki: 彼らはあなたの祖父母ですか？

Kate: そうよ。金婚式なのよ！　もう70代です。20代の早いころに結婚をしたの、50年以上前よ。(実際は50年を超えている)

Maki: バリーおじさんの写真はあるの？　よく話しているでしょ。

Kate: 実はね、実のおじは15年前に亡くなっているの。バリーは実のおじではないんだけど、子供のころからの知り合いなの。これがバリーよ。

Maki: すごく若く見えるわね。30代でしょ。

Kate: いやいや！　彼は1950年代に生まれているから、もう60代でしょう。時間がたつのは本当に早いわね！

WORDS & EXPRESSIONS

- **grandparents** 名祖父母　参 **grandchild** 孫
- **decade** 名10年
- **uncle** 名おじ　参 **aunt** おば
- **must be** ～に違いない　※"断定"を表す助動詞
- **How time flies!** 時のたつのは早い

Exploring grammar

> 期間に関する表現に使う
> since（〜以来）、for（〜の間）、ago（〜前に）など

We have known each other since we were high school students.
我々は高校生の時からの知り合いだ
☞ since の後には、〈主語＋動詞〉、名詞、副詞などがくる。

So, we have been together for such a long time.
だからすごい長い間のつき合いだ

Yes, we got to know about 30 years ago.
知り合ったのは30年前だね

Five years have passed since my uncle died.
おじが亡くなってから5年になる

期間を表すforを用いて言い換えると……
↓
My uncle has been dead for five years.
おじが亡くなって5年になる

過去形で表すと……
↓
My uncle died five years ago. おじは5年前に亡くなった
参 die の婉曲表現は **pass away**「亡くなる」

He has been a good boy since childhood.
彼は子供のころから良い子だ

"Since when have you been so polite?" "Since always!"
「いったいいつからそんなに上品なの？」「昔からだよ」

Her husband passed away when she was 25. She has been single since then.
彼女が25歳のときに夫が亡くなった。彼女はそれ以来ずっと一人だ

The pavilion was burnt down in 1800's and has since been rebuilt.
その別館は1800年代に焼け落ちて、その後再建されました

Barry returned to the State of Iowa, and I haven't seen him since.
バリーはアイオワ州に戻った、そしてそれ以来会っていない

They got married in spite of their parents' objection. But they have been happy ever since.
親の反対にもかかわらず結婚したが、彼らはその後ずっと幸せだ

● for は期間を示す。

for ages　長い間　　**for two decades**　20年間
for three centuries　3世紀の間
I haven't seen you for ages.　ずいぶん久しぶりだね
參 口語では **Long time no see.**　おひさしぶり

The tribe was in power for almost a century.
その部族はほぼ1世紀の間権力を握っていた

He traveled in the wilderness for half a year.
彼らは半年の間荒野を旅した

● 過去の時を表す ago

They got married 50 years ago, so this year they are going to celebrate their golden anniversary.
彼らは50年前に結婚したので、今年金婚式を祝います

Mom went out a few minutes ago.
ママはほんの少し前に出かけました　➡ Unit 24 参照
参 Mom has just gone out.

☛ "過去完了形" の文の中では ago の代わりに before を用いることに注意。

The family had moved to the new town five years before.
一家はすでに5年前に新しい町に引っ越してしまっていた

●「～代」を表す。

My second son left home in his teens.
次男は10代で家を出た

These days, many women do not get married in their twenties.
最近は20代で結婚しない女性が多い

参 in one's thirties　30代で（**in one's 30s** とも表記する）
　　年号の場合は **in the 1900s, in the 1900's**　1900年代に
　　　　　　　　in the 60s　60年代に

STRATEGIES FOR THE TOEIC

CAN YOU REMEMBER...?

- **Use these words to fill the blanks.**

  in / for / ago / since

1. _____ when have you been so polite?
2. My uncle has been dead _____ five years.
3. My second son left home _____ his teens.
4. They got married 50 years _____.
5. I haven't seen you _____ ages.
6. These days, many women do not get married _____ their twenties.

CAN YOU GUESS...?

- **Fill the blanks with words from this unit.**

7. The TV was invented in _____ early 1900s.
8. It was more than 20 years _____ when I last saw my old teacher.
9. My children are all in _____ twenties, now.
10. I've been studying English _____ many years.

ANSWERS

1 Since   2 for   3 in   4 ago   5 for   6 in   7 the
8 ago   9 their   10 for

UNIT 29 Verbs (2)

- ㊼ **Negative verbs** … 動詞の否定
- ㊽ **Adjective + verb** … 形容詞+動詞

LISTEN & READ

John's colleague, Makoto, has some bad news.

Makoto: John, ㊼**I don't know how to say this,** but I think we might not be going on that business trip to Hawaii next week.

John: You're kidding! How come?

Makoto: According to the boss, ㊽**it's necessary to make cuts** because of the economic situation.

John: ㊼**He doesn't realize** how important this trip is! I'll talk to him.

Makoto: You know how stubborn he is. I think it's ㊽**impossible to persuade** him to change his mind.

John: ㊼**I hadn't expected this.** Anyway, on the bright side, I'll have more time to practice my golf swing!

NOTES

- ☐ **How come?**　どうして
    - 同 = **Why?**　※用法 (語順) には注意。
        - 例 **How come you are so stubborn?**　君はどうしてそんなに頑固なんだ
            - ※S+Vの語順を取る。
        - 同 = **Why are you so stubborn?**

- ☐ **realize**　理解する・気づく
    - 参 イギリス綴りは **realise**

動詞 (2)

TRANSLATION

ジョンの同僚の誠が悪い知らせを伝えます。

Makoto: ジョン、どう言ってよいのか分からないけど、来週のハワイへの出張は行けないかもしれないんだ。

John: 冗談だろ！　どうしてだい？

Makoto: ボスが言うには、経済状況のために（経費を）切り詰める必要があるんだ。

John: ボスにはこの出張の大切さが分からないんだ。僕がボスに話すよ。

Makoto: 彼が頑固なのは知っているだろ。彼を説得して、考え直させるのは不可能だよ。

John: こんなこと予想もしてなかったよ。ともかく、明るく考えれば、ゴルフスイングの時間がもっととれるだろうよ。

WORDS & EXPRESSIONS

- **business trip**　出張
- **You're kidding!**　冗談だろ　参 **You must be kidding.** とも言う。
- **according to ~**　～によると・～が言うには
- **be necessary to ~**　～する必要がある
- **make cuts**　（経費・人件費などを）切り詰める
- **economic situation**　経済・財務状況
- **stubborn**　形 頑固な
- **persuade**　動 説得する
- **on the bright side**　明るい面を挙げれば・救われるのは
- **golf swing**　ゴルフスイング

EXPLORING GRAMMAR

〈It is 形容詞＋to 不定詞〉の構文

● 一般的なことを述べる場合に使う形容詞

necessary、**important**、**convenient**（便利な）、**dangerous**、**difficult**、**easy**、**hard**（困難な）、**possible**、**impossible**、**safe** などがある。

It is necessary to put an end to this stupidity.
この馬鹿さ加減に終止符を打つことが必要だ

● "意味上の主語" を明示する場合は〈for＋人〉にする。

① "客観的な必要性" や "可能・不可能" を表す

It is necessary for any of the attendees to reconcile different points of view on the issue.
出席者の誰にとってもこの問題に関する意見の相違を調整することが必要だ

It is impossible to finish this report in one day.
このレポートを1日で完成するのは不可能だ

② "相手に何かを勧めたり" "行動の必要性" などを述べる場合

advisable（望ましい）、**better**、**best**、**essential**（不可欠な）、**important**（重要だ）、**unnecessary**（不必要だ）などの形容詞が使われる。

It would be advisable for you to prepare for your thesis as soon as possible.
君ができるだけ早く論文の準備をするのが望ましいだろう

Wouldn't it be better for me to make an appointment with the professor right away?
すぐに教授にアポを取ったほうが良くありませんか

● 人間の性格や行為について"褒めたり""貶したり"する場合

① 〈It is 形容詞＋of ～＋to 不定詞〉の構文で意味上の主語を of で導く。

courageous（勇敢な）、**careless**（不注意）、**cruel**（冷酷な）、**generous**（気前がいい）、**kind**、**nice**、**sweet**、**good**（親切な・優しい）、**mean**（卑劣な）、**rude**、**impolite**（無礼な）、**absurd**、**stupid**、**silly**、**foolish**（バカな）、**sensible**（分別がある）などが使われる。

It was brave of my boyfriend to protect me from the burglar.
強盗から私を守ってくれるなんて彼は勇敢だったわ

It is generous of him to pay for the dinner for all of us.
みんなのディナー代を払ってくれるなんて彼は気前が良いわ

Isn't it stupid of me to turn down her offer?
彼女の申し出を断るなんてバカだよね？

It is so kind of you! How nice / sweet of you!
☛ Thank you very much. の代わりにこう言うこともできる。

It was so mean of him to criticize you without any good reasons.
ちゃんとした理由もなしに君を批判するなんて彼は卑劣だね

How careless of you (it is) to turn in the wrong thesis!
間違った論文を提出するなんて君はなんて不注意なんだ

It is easy to bake this kind of cake.
この種のケーキは焼くのが簡単だ

　　構文を変えて……
　　↓
This kind of cake is easy to bake.

と言うこともできる。

It is dangerous to drive this clunker.
こんなおんぼろ車を運転するのは危険だ

　　構文を変えて……
　　↓

This clunker is dangerous to drive.

● 次の 2 つの文を比べてみよう。

1. It is good for you to stop smoking.
禁煙すると体に良い

2. It was good of you to give me a hand.
手伝ってくれてありがとう

　　1. の **good** は「健康に良い」という客観的な表現で、
　　2. の **good** は **kind**、**sweet**、**nice** と同じ意味である。

否定のいろいろ

● not、never を用いて文の内容を否定する。

Most of the students do not like their school uniforms.
学生のほとんどが制服が好きではない

I have never been to Spain in my life.
今までにスペインには行ったことがない

Never has he told a lie.　彼は嘘をついたことが全くない

I didn't expect her to show up at the party.
彼女がパーティーに顔を出すとは期待していなかった

- not が語、句、節を否定する。

   I signed up for English class, not math class.
   私が登録したのは英語の授業で、数学の授業ではありません
   - 🡆 not は math class という語（句）を否定している。

   I am here on business, not for pleasure.
   私は仕事で来ているんです、遊びじゃないんです
   - 🡆 not は for pleasure という句を否定している

   It was not because she was pretty that I asked her out.
   彼女をデートに誘ったのは彼女がかわいかったからではないのです
   - 🡆 not は because she was pretty という節を否定している。

- 否定の節の代わりをする not

   "Will it rain heavily tomorrow?" 明日雨はひどいでしょうか

   "I hope not." 降らないといいけど
   - 🡆 not は "it will not rain heavily tomorrow" という節の代わりをしている。
   - 参 **I'm afraid so.** 残念ながら降るだろう

   "We are going to give a party. Can you make it?"
   パーティーをやるんだけど、来られるかい

   "I'm afraid not." 残念だけどむり
   - 🡆 not は "I can't make it / I can't come to the party" の代わりをしている。

● 否定を強める表現

not ~ at all 全く〜ない　**not ~ in the lease** すこしも〜ない
can't / couldn't possibly~ とても〜できない／できなかった

"Do you mind my sitting on this seat?" "No, not at all."
「この席に座っても構いませんか」「ええ、もちろんどうぞ」
　☞ mind は "気にする" という意味なので、「構わない」は "気にしない" となる。
　　従って "少しも気にしない" が「はい、どうぞ」になる。（既習）

She was not in the least nervous when she appeared on the stage.
彼女は舞台に現れたとき、全く緊張していなかった

● その他の否定

None、Nobody、Neither、No など

None of my friends came to ask after me when I was in hospital.
入院中友人のだれも見舞いに来なかった

Nobody told me the news.
誰も私にそれを知らせてくれなかった

He didn't ask for help. Neither did she.
彼は助けを求めなかった。彼女も（求めなかった）

Neither of my brothers likes to play golf.
二人の兄弟はいずれもゴルフをしたがらない

None of your business! 大きなお世話だ

Strategies for the TOEIC

Can you remember...?

- **For questions 1 to 4 use these words to fill the blanks.**

  verbs: pay / finish / criticize / bake
  adjectives: generous / easy / impossible / mean

1. It is _____ this report in one day.
2. It is _____ him _____ for the dinner for all of us.
3. It was so _____ him _____ you without any good reasons.
4. It is _____ this kind of cake.
5. She was not in (a / the) least nervous when she appeared on the stage.
6. He didn't ask for help. _____ did she.

Can you guess...?

- **Choose the correct word or words in brackets ( ).**

7. It was not because you arrived late (so / that / then) I was angry.
8. "Do we have a test today?" "I hope (no / don't / not)."
9. His books are so easy (to read / for reading).
10. What a surprise! I (didn't / hadn't / don't) expect to get promoted!

Answers

1. impossible to finish   2. generous of, to pay   3. mean of, to criticize
4. easy to bake   5. the   6. Neither   7. that   8. not   9. to read
10. didn't

UNIT 30 Verbs (3)

- ㊾ Reduced infinitive … 代不定詞
- ㊿ Verb + gerund / infinitive … 動詞＋動名詞／不定詞

LISTEN & READ

The Browns are discussing their plans for their last day in Japan.

Trevor: How about going to Ueno zoo? ㊾**I've been wanting to** since we arrived.

Emily: ㊾**I don't want to!** I'd like to go shopping in Ginza! Don't you want to go to Ginza, Mom?

Angela: ㊾**I'd love to!** ㊿**I was thinking of buying** a nice souvenir for gran.

Georgie: ㊾**I don't want to!** I want to go to the zoo with dad!

Trevor: Angela, ㊿**this shirt wants ironing**. What shall I do?

Angela: Well, why don't you wear a different shirt to go to the zoo with Georgie and I'll buy you a new one when I go shopping with Emily?

Trevor: Excellent idea! Georgie, get ready to see the lions!

NOTES

- **How about ~ing?**　〜するのはどうですか　意見を聞く表現
  ※「〜してはどうですか」と勧める場合にも用いる。
- **Why don't you wear a different shirt?**　違うシャツを着たらどうですか
  参 How about ~ing?　同〈Why don't you + V?〉
- **a new one**　one は a new shirt の代名詞表現

動詞 (3)

TRANSLATION

ブラウン家の人たちは日本での最終日の計画について話し合っています。

Trevor: 上野動物園に行くのはどうですか？ （日本に）着いてからずっと行きたいと思っていたんだ。

Emily: 私は行きたくないわ！ 銀座でショッピングをしたいの。お母さん、銀座に行きたくない？

Angela: 行きたいわよ！ おばあちゃんに素敵なお土産を買おうと思っていたのよ。

Georgie: 僕は行きたくないよ！ お父さんと動物園に行きたい！

Trevor: アンジェラ、このシャツはアイロンをかけないといけないよ。どうしよう？

Angela: そうね、ジョージーと動物園に行くのには違うシャツを着ていったらどうなの、エミリーとショッピングに行ったときに新しいのを買うわ。

Trevor: 素晴らしい考えだね！ ジョージー、ライオンさんに会う準備をしなさい！

WORDS & EXPRESSIONS

- **souvenir** 名 お土産
- **gran** 名 おばあちゃん（英：幼児語）
  参 米語では grandma, grandmother のこと。
     gramp / grampa　おじいちゃん
- **excellent** 形 素晴らしい
- **get ready** 準備する、用意をする

EXPLORING GRAMMAR

代不定詞

● 重複を避けるために to 不定詞の代わりに to だけで表現することがある。

動詞

hope、**hate**、**intend**（～するつもりだ）、**want**、**would like**、**would love**、**mean**（つもりだ≒intend）、**plan**（計画している）、**try** など。

助動詞

have、**need**、**ought** や **used to**、**be able to**、**be going to** などにも見られる。

A: **Sally, would you like to go out with me tonight?**
サリー、今夜デートしないか

B: **I'd love to, but I have so much homework to catch up on.**
そうしたいのだけど。遅れている宿題がたくさんあるの

A: **Did you buy the textbook, Sandy?**
サンディ、教科書は買いましたか

B: **No, I tried to, but I didn't know where to buy it.**
買おうとしたんですが、どこで買えるのか分からなかったのです

A: **Do you play the guitar?** ギターは弾きますか

B: **Not now, but I used to.** 今は弾かないよ。昔は弾いたけどね

A: **Have you finished cleaning your room?**
部屋の掃除は終わったかい

B: **No, I know I ought to, but I have to go to my part-time job now.**
いや。やらなくてはいけないことは分かっているんだけど、バイトに行かなくてはいけないんだ

I wanted to go to the Adele concert, but I wasn't able to.
アデルのコンサートに行きたかったんだけど、行けなかった

I'm very busy for the moment, but I will do what I have to.
今のところすごく忙しいんだけど、やらなくてはいけないことはやるよ

A: **Yumeka, have you done your homework yet?**
夢花、宿題はもう終わったの

B: **No, but I'm just going to.** ううん、今やろうと思ったのに

☞ Dialogue にある、No, I don't want to.「(そう) したくない」のように否定する場合もある。

● 「〜しようかと思っている」はいろいろな構文で表現できる。

I am thinking of studying abroad some day.
いつか留学しようと思っている

☞ I think to 不定詞の構文はないので、be thinking of ~ing を用いる。

I intend to major in psychology. 心理学を専攻するつもりだ

I'm planning to take / make a trip to San Francisco.
サンフランシスコに旅行する計画だ

I'm going to write a poem about rain. 雨の詩を書くつもりだ

I have been wanting to go to the zoo.
長い間動物園に行きたかった (気持を表している)

過去形にすると……
↓
I was thinking of taking a bath first.
先にお風呂に入ろうと思っていた

とすると "実現していない" 感じになる。

221

能動受動態

● 形は能動態だが意味は受動態の文

This machine needs oiling.　この機械は油をさす必要がある
☛ machine からすれば、"油をさされる"わけだが能動態の動名詞を用いる。もちろん This machine needs to be oiled. も文としては正しいが、needs oiling が慣用。

Nara is worth paying a visit to.　奈良は訪問する価値がある
同 **It is worthwhile to pay a visit to / visit Nara.**

This shirt wants washing.　このシャツは洗わなくてはいけない

Your hair wants combing.　髪をとかした方がいいよ

などいくつかの慣用表現に見られる。

● 動名詞の表現ではないが、

Yohkai Watch books sell well.　妖怪ウオッチの本はよく売れる
☛ このことから"一番売れる本"を best-seller と言うことがわかるだろう。
参 **seller** は「本屋さん」ではなく「本」のこと。

This dress washes well.　このドレスは洗いがきく

STRATEGIES FOR THE TOEIC

• Fill the blanks with words from this unit, or use the verbs in brackets.

CAN YOU REMEMBER...?

1. "Sally, would you like to go out with me tonight?"
   "I _____, but I have so much homework to catch up on."

2. "Did you buy the textbook, Sandy?" "No, I _____, but I didn't know where to buy it."

3. "Do you play the guitar?" "Not now, but I _____."

4. I _____ studying abroad some day.   (think)

5. I _____ major in psychology.   (intend)

6. This machine _____ oiling.

CAN YOU GUESS...?

7. I've been (want / wanted / wanting) to see that movie for a long time.

8. Your car (wants / is wanting / is wanted) repairing.

9. It's worth (to pay / paying / having paid) a visit to Bath, if you have time.

10. I don't know my teacher's name, though I (ought to / ought know).

ANSWERS

1. would love to   2. tried to   3. used to   4. am thinking of
5. intend to   6. needs   7. wanting   8. wants   9. paying
10. ought to

Review 3

Fill the blanks. Use the words in brackets ( ) to help you.
If the words are separated by a slash (/), choose the correct word or words.

Grammar Keys 35 ~ 38

A. I asked him how much it _____ (would cost / will cost / costs) to renovate our apartment.

B. I thought you _____ (want / are wanting / wanted) to renovate the place.

C. You _____ me that there wasn't enough space for your desk and you _____ you needed a bigger office! (told / talked / spoke / said)

D. I passed my driver's test! _____ (have) it not been for your help and support, I _____ (not pass).

E. Oh, if only I _____ (have) a rich boyfriend. Then he _____ (can) buy me a sports car!

Grammar Keys 39 ~ 44

F. I _____ (took / was taking / had taken) a nap when you came in. I didn't hear you.

224   Review 3

G. We _____ (be) to lots of interesting places, but we _____ (not be) to Kyoto yet.

H. I'm a novelist. I _____ (write) stories since I was a child.

I. Ugh! This milk _____ (is tasting / has tasted / tastes) sour!

J. I _____ (not know) that you _____ (live) in New York before _____ (move) to Tokyo!

K. I practice at a golf range two or three times _____ week and play on a full course once _____ month. (on / a / for / in)

🗝 Grammar Keys ㊺ ~ ㊿

L. I've known him _____ (since / for / ago) I was a child.

M. They got married in _____ (there / they're / their) early twenties, over fifty years _____ (since / for / ago)!

N. He _____ (not realize) how important this trip is!

O. I think it's impossible _____ (to persuade / in persuading) him to change his mind.

225

Review 3

P. How about going to Ueno zoo? I've been wanting _____ (it / to) since we arrived.

Q. I was thinking _____ (of buying / to buy) a nice souvenir for gran.

Answer Key

A. I asked him how much it <u>would cost</u> to renovate our apartment.

B. I thought you <u>wanted</u> to renovate the place.

C. You <u>told</u> me that there wasn't enough space for your desk and you <u>said</u> you needed a bigger office!

D. <u>Had</u> it not been for your help and support, I <u>wouldn't have passed</u>.

E. Oh, if only I <u>had</u> a rich boyfriend. Then he <u>could</u> buy me a sports car!

F. I <u>was taking</u> a nap when you came in.

G. We<u>'ve been</u> to lots of interesting places, but we <u>haven't been</u> to Kyoto yet.

H. I<u>'ve been writing</u> stories since I was a child.

I. This milk <u>tastes</u> sour!

J. I <u>didn't know</u> that you <u>had lived</u> in New York before <u>moving (you moved)</u> to Tokyo!

K. I practice at a golf range two or three times <u>a</u> week and play on a full course once <u>a</u> month.

L. I've known him <u>since</u> I was a child.

M. They got married in <u>their</u> early twenties, over fifty years <u>ago</u>!

N. He <u>doesn't realize</u> how important this trip is!

O. I think it's impossible <u>to persuade</u> him to change his mind.

P. I've been wanting <u>to</u> since we arrived.

Q. I was thinking <u>of buying</u> a nice souvenir for gran.

装丁：	PARK. Sutherland Inc.
本文デザイン：	ドルフィン
イラスト：	高橋正輝
ナレーター：	Josh Keller, Deirdre Merrell-Ikeda, Kimberly Tierney
録音スタジオ：	株式会社　巧芸創作

コミュミケーションのための
やり直し英文法

2015年2月6日　第1刷発行

著　者　　草野　進
　　　　　スティーブ・リア

発行者　　浦　晋亮

発行所　　IBCパブリッシング株式会社
　　　　　〒162-0804 東京都新宿区中里町29番3号 菱秀神楽坂ビル9F
　　　　　Tel. 03-3513-4511　Fax. 03-3513-4512
　　　　　www.ibcpub.co.jp

印刷所　　株式会社シナノパブリッシングプレス

© 草野進，スティーブ・リア 2015
Printed in Japan

落丁本・乱丁本は、小社宛にお送りください。送料小社負担にてお取り替えいたします。
本書の無断複写（コピー）は著作権法上での例外を除き禁じられています。

ISBN978-4-7946-0325-8